Yorkshire

The crimes behind the Hangings

1864 – 1910

In remembrance of all the innocent lives that were lost,
so enabling this publication to be written.

www.yorkshire-executions.co.uk

The crimes behind the hangings

Yorkshire Executions

First edition published in 2009

© Copyright 2009

Ian Charles

The rights of Ian Charles to be identified as the author of this work has been asserted by him in accordance with the Copyright, Design and Patents Act 1998.

All rights reserved. No reproduction, copy or transmission of this publication in part or whole, may be made without express prior written permission.

No paragraph of this publication may be reproduced, copied or transmitted except with the express prior written permission or in accordance with the provisions of the Copyright Act 1956 (amended).

Any person who commits any unauthorised act in relation to this publication may be liable to criminal prosecution and civil claims for damage.

Although every effort has been made to ensure the accuracy of the information contained in this book the author or the publisher can be held liable for any erratum.

ISBN 978-09561480-1-8

Published by David Firth

www.yorkshire-executions.co.uk

With thanks to all whom helped in the preparation of this book.

A special thank you to:

Dr. 'frothy' Firth

Gary Pearson aka. Lord Bubbles of Bubbles-shire

And lastly, but most importantly:

Tonya

For your continued support, with editing, proof reading, researching and putting up with me over the months while writing the book.

www.yorkshire-executions.co.uk

The crimes behind the hangings

Prologue

H.M.P. Leeds, formerly known as Leeds gaol or jail and locally known as the Armley nick. Was opened in July 1847, at a cost of £43,000, which included purchase of the land and the construction costs. It stands quite impressively, high in the skyline a mile west of the town centre.

Architect's Perkins and Backhouse designed the prison similar to all the other new Victorian penitentiary principles, a centre with four wings branching off facing the points of the compass. There are three floors to each wing and cells along both sides.

Originally built to house 334 men and women, the first inmate was James Beaumont.

Over recent years the prison has been modernised and extended, it can now house well in excess of 1000 prisoners, most of who are on remand awaiting trial, and those whom have been sentenced by the courts and are awaiting allocation to various prisons within the prison service. It took over the duty of executions from York castle for the West Riding convicts. York castle still executed prisoners from the North Riding Assizes.

The first execution and the only public hanging was performed in 1864, just outside the prison walls, this strangely was a double hanging, one of only 8 carried out at the prison. (Strangely enough, another first, in 1903 the only female prisoner to be hanged at Armley gaol was also executed in double hanging)

The bricked up tunnel in the boundary walls, where the first two men to be publicly hanged walked through to the hanging field, to be greeted by the hangman Thomas Askern, and to meet their fate, can still be seen clearly today. 80,000 spectators turned out to witness this event at 9am on the 10th September 1864.

York castle jail formerly known at the Debtors prison was opened in 1704 taking 4 years to build. In 1773 a courthouse was built at the side of the prison, then later in 1783 a female prison was built to the other side. The prisons closed at the end of the 19th century, they were renovated and now are open to the public as the Castle museum. The courtroom still officiates as the York crown court; the prisoners while waiting for their trial are still locked up in the original cells.

Between 1864 – 1910, 59 convicts were to be hanged. 40 at Armley, 10 at York the last one being in 1896, then due to the prison closing, Hull and Wakefield prisons took over. Hull executed 5 prisoners and Wakefield 4 between these years.

Between the sentence and the execution.

After the prisoner was found guilty of the capital offence and sentenced to death, they would be taken straight to the prison that would perform the execution. The Assizes at Leeds would send the prisoner straight to Armley jail, and York prisoners would be sent next door to the castle jail. When York castle jail closed around 1900 the prisoners would be transferred either to Hull or Wakefield, this would depend on the location of their crimes.

The prisoner would be placed in a special cell, known as the Condemned Cell, the light would be on 24 hrs a day, and the prisoner would be guarded by a team of warders. The warders tried to occupy the prisoner throughout the 2 or 3 weeks between sentence and the execution, they were allowed to comfort them and would play cards, chess or draughts with them. Everything that the prisoner had to say would be recorded in case something was mentioned like a vital piece of evidence or an admission of guilt. The warders were also there for the purpose of preventing the prisoner from attempting suicide.

The prisoner would be segregated from the other prisoners and were able to receive visits from family and friends. The prison chaplain would also be at hand to administer religious teachings. The Sunday before the execution they would attend Sunday service in the chapel, a prayer would be said for their soul, they would though be kept out of site of the other prisoners.

The governor of the prison would be required by law to be available at anytime night or day for the prisoner to speak to, if the prisoner wished. He would a day or two before the execution have to unpleasant task of informing the prisoner whether a reprieve had been granted or not.

Meanwhile the High Sheriff of the county would have set the date of the execution. He would appoint the executioner and his assistant and make sure all the preparations were ready for the allocated day, regardless of whether a reprieve might be granted. Even though 49% of prisoners were reprieved, the execution would have to be ready to proceed in necessary on the date arranged.

The judge had to pass the sentence of death on all capital crimes; he could though make a recommendation whether the sentence should be carried out or not.

The Home Office would be sent the case papers of the trial, along with the judge's recommendation. A report would then be sent to the Home Secretary, who then would decide whether the execution would go ahead or issue a Royal Prerogative of Mercy on behalf of the monarch and reprieve the prisoner.

If a sentence was to go ahead he would right on the file 'the law must take its course'. He would then write to the governor of the prison, who had to task of informing the prisoner. There were no set rules whether to grant a reprieve to a prisoner, most jury's recommended mercy, this normally had no bearing on the Home Secretary's decision, but if the judge in his report recommendation a reprieve, this would normally be granted. Capital offences committed by poisoning would rarely be reprieved, as this would be normally seen as premeditated.

The prisoner would have had enormous mental pressure on their shoulders, anxiously wondering whether they were going to be reprieved or if they were to meet a long slow death by strangulation. Once the governor informed them of the Home Secretary's decision of a reprieve, more often than not the prisoner would have to spend time in the prisons medical wing to overcome the stress, before joining the general population of the prisoner. The one's which didn't get reprieved would normally turn to religious administrations and prepare mentally for the execution.

The afternoon before the execution, the executioner and his assistant would arrive at the jail, they would view the prisoner in his cell secretly, this helped them to judge the length of the drop.

The rope would be stretched over night, to remove any elastically from it. They would stay in the prison that night, then accompany the governor and chaplain to the Condemned Cell in the morning.

The prisoner was allowed to wear his own clothes, and would if necessary allowed a glass of Brandy prescribed by the prison doctor to steady the nerves.

The governor would give them the signal to go ahead and then the executioner would take over. He and his assistant would walk into the cell, pinion the prisoner's hands and legs then walk with them to the gallows. A white hood would be placed over the prisoner's head, the rope put round their neck and the bolt drawn. Thus sending the prisoner falling through the trap and executed.

The prison bells would begin to toll fifteen minutes before the execution and fifteen minutes after, if the prison didn't have a bell, the local church bells would be used.

This was not to tell the local residents that an execution was taking place, but it was to scare away the evil sprits from the departed. The newly dead were in great danger, for hordes of these evil sprits were believed to by laying in wait to seize the souls of the dead. It was assumed that the devil hated the sounds of the bells, as this was the sound that called people to church to pray.

After the bolt was pulled and the prisoner had dropped, the doctor would listen to the fading heartbeat, once the heart had stopped; he would pronounce the prisoner dead. A black flag was raised, to show that the execution had been successful and a notice would be placed on the prison gates saying:

DECLARATION OF THE GOVERNOR

"I, the undersigned, declare that judgement of death was this day executed on (prisoner) in Armley in my presence."

The body would be left suspended for an hour before being taken down, and an autopsy performed, followed by an inquest. The body would be placed naked in to a wooden coffin, then wheeled to the north side of the prison. It would then be taken out of the coffin, placed in an unmarked grave, covered in a shawl and then buried. The north side of the prison was used as the sun doesn't shine on that side of the prison, and allegedly that ground belongs to the devil and was the domain of the evil sprits.

Up until 1888, the executioner would have been responsible for supplying the rope, which he was allowed to keep after the execution. He was also allowed to keep the prisoners clothes that would more often than not be sold as souvenirs.

No training was needed for the role of executioner, just a strong stomach. Most of the early executioners would be criminals themselves, applying for the role from inside the prison population. Thomas Askern was one such case; he was in York castle jail when he applied of hanging William Dove at York in 1856.

Incidentally Dick Turpin the infamous highwayman, murderer and horse thief was executed on the 7th April 1739 at York. Thomas Hadfield who just happened to have been in Turpin's gang, and was also in prison waiting to be executed, hanged him. Hadfield was pardoned provided that he acted in the capacity of the executioner.

After 1892 the executioners had to officially apply for any vacant position and had a week's training course. They had to sign the official Secrets Act; therefore they couldn't disclose any details of the execution.
1901 saw the rules on the ringing of the bells changed, the bell now was rung only after the execution was completed. In 1902 the customary flying of the black flag was abolished.

Chapters

	Title	Execution Location	Date
1	Quick Myers	Armley	10/09/1864
2	The Reward	Armley	10/09/1864
3	Former Inmates	York	04/04/1868
4	The Little Sister	York	18/08/1874
5	Sheffield Knife Maker	Armley	21/02/1875
6	Ruined Christmas	Armley	03/04/1877
7	The Ship's Carpenter	York	15/04/1878
8	Master Of Disguise	Armley	25/02/1879
9	Leeds Gamekeeper	York	27/05/1879
10	The Cracked Watch	York	11/05/1881
11	The Sheffield Cutler	Armley	23/05/1881
12	Rising Sun	Armley	25/05/1882
13	The Gleaner	York	28/11/1882
14	Don't Do It Dadda!	Armley	26/08/1884
15	Dodworth Poacher	York	09/11/1886
16	The Ex Employee	Armley	22/08/1887
17	A Broken Brush	Armley	22/05/1888
18	Huddersfield Groom	Armley	01/01/1889
19	The Showman	Armley	31/12/1889
20	Railwayman	Armley	31/12/1889
21	Bowling Murder	Armley	26/08/1890
22	Police Killer	York	30/12/1890
23	Gruesome Murder	Armley	18/08/1891
24	The Barmaid	Armley	05/01/1892
25	Holbeck Murder	Armley	14/06/1892
26	Battered To death	Armley	18/08/1892
27	The Hatchet	Armley	04/04/1893
28	Low Meadows	Armley	03/04/1894
29	Baby Poisoner	Armley	21/08/1894
30	Helmsley Holiday	York	13/08/1895
31	A Shilling	Armley	31/12/1895
32	The Sailor	Armley	25/08/1896
33	Swedish Sailor	York	22/12/1896
34	Family Robinson	Armley	17/08/1897
35	30 Minute Trial	Armley	17/08/1897

The crimes behind the hangings

36	2 Little Girls	Armley	16/08/1900
37	P.C. Kew	Armley	16/08/1900
38	Two Trials	Armley	28/08/1900
39	Auntie Sarah	Hull	25/03/1902
40	Oh! Bill	Hull	23/12/1902
41	Farm Hands	Hull	22/12/1903
42	Good Morning John	Armley	29/12/1903
43	The Poachers	Armley	29/02/1904
44	Middlesbrough Killer	Armley	29/03/1904
45	Voices In My Head	Armley	17/08/1904
46	York Murder	Armley	20/12/1904
47	The Plasterer	Armley	15/08/1905
48	49 Stabs	Armley	18/12/1905
49	Wakefield's 1st	Wakefield	10/04/1906
50	Middlesbrough Strangler	Wakefield	09/08/1906
51	Last Journey	Hull	04/08/1908
52	The Reference	Armley	03/12/1908
53	Christmas Murder	Wakefield	02/03/1909
54	Crock's Yard	Armley	12/03/1909
55	The Painter	Wakefield	09/07/1909
56	The Sister In Law	Hull	07/12/1909
57	The Summons	Armley	09/08/1910
58	Was It A fall?	Armley	29/12/1910

Chapter 1 - Quick Myers

Joseph Myers was a 44-year-old jovial fellow on the rare occasion that he was sober. Having for years led a corrupt life and having participated in brutal sports. Living with Alice his wife in a sparsely furnished house in Sheffield he had a history of physically abusing her. He had assaulted Alice so atrociously previously, that he had been sentenced to a spell in prison.

When he put his mind to work he was one of the best saw sharpeners in the North of England. He could quite easy earn £6 or £7 a week, which was a huge amount of money back in 1864. He often worked 2 days then spent 3 days drinking. His cleverness as a workman gave him the nickname of 'quick'. Most people knew him by his nickname rather than his proper name.

His drinking and violence was so bad that he was feared in the local public houses, many people left the pub in terror as soon he entered.

Alice was the complete opposite of her husband; her neighbours and friends would describe her as hardworking, patient, honest, good-natured and a reasonably good-tempered woman. She had petitioned the prison authorities to secure the early release of her husband and eventually this proved to be successful.

Myers was released on a licence not to commit further offences, carry a weapon or assault his wife. If he broke any law he would be sent straight back to prison to complete his sentence. He returned to their Sheffield home, but the stern warning from the court was not heeded, he continued to beat Alice with even more violence than he had in the past.

Like most couples arguments and the exchange of angry words would often occur between them. Myers was overheard saying that as soon as his license was finished in a fortnight she would not live another hour.

On the morning of the murder, Alice was said to have not been in her usual calm humour that she had often been credited with.

The crimes behind the hangings

Myers had been drinking heavily, Alice had been busy doing the washing, and she went out to the yard to hang the washing out to dry. Myers followed and a heated exchange of words ensued.

Alice went back into the house closely followed by Myers. In a fit of rage Myers picked up a pair of scissors and attacked Alice, stabbing her in the face, neck, shoulder and breast. Filled with instant remorse he made a feeble attempt at suicide, using a table knife he slashed his throat.

Myers' daughter and son-in-law arrived at the house to find Mrs. Myers in a pool of blood in the kitchen, and Myers upstairs in the bedroom covered in blood.

The police were called and Myers either through genuine remorse or boasting said, "Give me the knife so I can finish myself."

He was taken to hospital, where he made another unsuccessful suicide bid, trying to throw himself out of a window. The surgeon with great skill managed to stitch the wound to his neck; Myers was expected to make a full recovery. He was taken from the hospital to the police station and charged with his wife's murder.

He pleaded guilty to murder and was sentenced to death at West Riding Assizes on August 17th, 1864.

On September 9th, the day before he was due to die, his two young children, his son-in-law and other relatives visited him. Blaming drink for his crime, he begged for their forgiveness. As they embraced him the prison chaplain asked them all to kneel and pray. "I swore I would never kneel." Said Myers, bursting into tears, "But I will do so now."

He was hanged the next day, Saturday, September 10th, 1864, alongside James Sargisson.

It turned out later that when Myers's brother came to visit him the day before the execution, he had actually shared the same carriage on the train as executioner Thomas Askern.

Chapter 2 - The Reward

John Cooper aged 26, was a garden worker and lived at Hansworth, Sheffield. On the 9th April 1864, he set off walking to visit his parent's home at Stone, which was roughly 13 miles away. He passed through a village called Laughton-Cum-Northern, Rotherham, and called in to the public house for refreshments.

At roughly 9pm he was asked for the time, he obliged in telling. Then at about 10pm he was asked the same question. Again he produced his watch from his pocket and proceeded to tell the time. A little while later he finished his drink and set of to continue the walk to his parents.

He never arrived and was found the next morning laid dead in a country lane near Roche Abbey. Next to the dead body was a fence post covered in blood. He had been badly beaten his watch, keys and a small amount of money missing.

A murder inquiry started, and upon investigation James Sargisson of Rotherham was identified as the man whom Cooper had been kind enough to pass on the time of day.

Sargisson was arrested and taken to the police station for questioning. Detective inspector Fisher of the West Riding constabulary interviewed Sargisson.

In a statement taken, Sargisson had said that he left the public house before the deceased and walked towards his home, about 100 yards away. He didn't enter his home but turned round and walked back past the pub, and along a path leading to Laughton. He had met a girl called Jane Hawke; they talked for a while before he continued his journey. There was no evidence at that time to press charges so Sargisson was released, while further enquires were made.

Detective inspectors Hockaday and Fisher carried out the investigation of the case, Jane Hawke was interviewed, she categorically denied speaking to or even seeing Sargisson that evening.

They also interviewed a young boy who had watched Cooper leave the public house that evening, and who had noticed a man stood opposite watching the pub door, dressed like, and looking similar to Sargisson. The man had then followed the victim down the lane towards Roche Abbey.

The licensee of the public house Mr. Mottram stated that Sargisson had been drinking in his establishment that evening, he left just before the victim. Another man William Taylor, one of Sargisson's drinking partners had also left at roughly the same time.

A neighbour living near the public house made a statement to the effect of on that particular evening she was waiting for her husband to return from work, when she heard footsteps walking past her house, closely followed by two more pairs of footsteps hurriedly going in the same direction.

It was then decided that Sargisson would be re-arrested and on the morning of 3rd May 1864, the police went to his father's address in Brookhouse where Sargisson was arrested.

A search of the house was conducted and under the mattress, which he slept; the police found a rolled up pair of trousers that were badly stained in what appeared to be blood. In a nearby pigsty a watch and bunch of keys were discovered. These were later identified as being the property of Cooper.

A couple of hours later, after the search was finally completed; Sargisson was interviewed and asked about the trousers. He commented that they were the ones that he had worn on the night of the murder. They had been washed but they hadn't come clean, so he had not worn them since.

He went on to say, "I left the beer house the evening just before the deceased left, I bumped into George Denton, who asked where I was going. I told him that I was going home. Then Cooper walked out of the public house; Denton asked me who he was. I replied that he was a stranger who was just passing through. Denton then asked me if I would accompany him on a walk to the nearby village of Slade Hooton. I agreed so we set off towards Roche Abbey that just happened to be in the same direction as Cooper. It was when we were out of sight of any houses, at a turn in the road; Denton picked up a fence post, walked over to Cooper and said I know you! At the same time hitting him over the right temple. Cooper immediately fell to the floor; Denton rifled through his pockets, found the watch, keys and some money. Denton said to me that he thought that the man was dead but lets make sure. He then started kicking him in about his head. Before we separated Denton gave me the watch and keys for safe keeping until he found a customer for them, Denton kept all the money himself."

The police officer's asked about the trousers, why had he washed and hid them if he had not committed the murder?

Sargisson's reply was that, during the scuffle Denton had lost his cap, he had been helping by rummaging around in the dark to find it, he had knelt in the blood that was gushing out of the dead mans head.

Upon the information received from Sargisson. Denton was apprehended in Sheffield, he denied that he had participated in the murder of Cooper. Both men where charged with murder and ordered to be tried at Leeds Assizes.

William Taylor, the man who left the public house shortly after Sargisson was also arrested, interviewed and charged with conspiracy to murder, these charges were later dropped at the committal hearing at the magistrates court. Sargisson had made a statement to the court, denying that Taylor wasn't even there.

Both Sargisson and Denton pleaded not guilty at the trial. Mr. Overend, Mr. Maude and Mr. Barker prosecuted the prisoners, Mr. Vernon Blackburn defended Denton, and Mr. Waddy defended Sargisson.

Denton's mother, whom he lived with, gave evidence that he was in bed at 9pm the evening of the murder, he did not leave the house again until 6 or 7 the next morning. The jury however found that the evidence did not support the attempt that Sargis-

The crimes behind the hangings

son had made to incriminate Denton, and the case against him was thrown out of court.

The judge in summing up the case against Sargisson pointed out to the jury that, persons who aided and assisted another person in the act of committing murder were also responsible, and were to be found guilty of murder.

The jury retired to consider the case and reach their verdict, almost immediately they returned to the courtroom and pronounced the accused guilty of murder.

Placing the black cap on his head the judge addressed Sargisson.

"You have been convicted of a very cruel and cowardly murder perpetrated by either you alone or in the company of some other man. You assailed this poor man on his way home, took his life without giving him any chance of defending himself. It only remains for me to pronounce sentence upon you."

The sentence of death was then passed in the normal way.

Sargisson placed his head in his hands and wept uncontrollably. He had to be removed from the dock while sobbing and protesting that he was as innocent as an unborn baby was.

He was taken to the condemned cell at Armley gaol to wait the date of his execution. It is rumoured though that he did try to escape, but was overpowered by wardens guarding him.

Between the sentence and the execution, no effort was made to save the life of Sargisson. His father and also a former employer visited him. He was asked if his denial of murder was true, he stuck to his story that he did not take part in any of the violence that was inflicted on Cooper. He had only implicated himself to being at the scene of the murder, so that he would be able to claim the reward offered for the capture of the murderer.

He also spoke to the Bishop of Ripon who said of Denton, "If I could say anything to free Denton from suspicion, I would, but he is guilty, he struck the fatal blow."

Sargisson was executed in the first ever execution performed at Armley gaol, a double execution along side Joseph Myers.

This was the first and only public execution; it became a local spectacle with over 80,000 people taking to the streets to watch Thomas Askern pull the lever of the trap outside the gaol in the hanging field.

As Askern placed the white hood over Sargisson's head, he cried out, "Are thou happy now lad." Directed at Denton.

It took 2 to 3 minutes for Sargisson to die, taking the truth of what really happened that night to his grave.

Chapter 3 – Former Inmates

The Beverley house of correction released two prisoners on the 29th February 1868, namely Daniel Driscoll and a couple of minutes later, 21 year old Frederick Parker. Each man were given their property at the gate, Driscoll was given, 4 gold sovereign's, 11 shillings, a silver watch, silver watch guard, a watch key, a trowel and other small items of property. Parker collected 1 shilling, 4d in money and postage stamps to the value of 4 shillings.

Before they were released they had arranged to meet up later that morning for a drink. They met at the Red Lion public house, in Beverley. They stayed and drank for a couple of hours, the landlord had noticed that Driscoll bought the ale all the time, Parker never once paid for a round of drinks.

During the afternoon Driscoll mentioned to the landlord that he had 4 gold sovereigns. Parker overheard this comment and not long afterwards, Driscoll looked at his watch, again Parker noticed this.

They left the Red Lion and were next seen 15 miles away at a public house in Bubwith. They arrived together at approximately 7pm, had a couple of drinks, Driscoll again paid.

When they were ready to leave Driscoll, said that he was going on to his parents at Hemmingbrough, both men then left the public house. They were never seen in each other's company again, in fact the body of Daniel Driscoll was found the next morning.

At 9am on the Sunday 1st March 1868, Mr. Jackson was walking down Cliffe Turnpike Road, 3 miles from Bubwith near Selby. He noticed a bundle of what appeared to be clothes at the side of the road, along side was a trowel. On further inspection this bundle of clothes was the dead body of which later was identified as Daniel Driscoll. Laid not far from the deceased was a large hedge stake splattered in blood.

The police were called, it was confirmed that the hedge stake was the weapon used to cause the severe wounds and fractured the skull of the deceased. The body had been robbed; the watch and chain were missing, as was the deceased money apart from 2d.

At around 8.45am that morning Parker arrived at a Mr. Bentley's house five miles from Bubwith. He had with him amongst other items, a silver watch and guard, and some money in both gold and silver coins. He told Mr. Bentley that he had just been released from Beverley jail, this was his property that the jail had given him on his release.

Mrs. Bentley noticed that the prisoner had blood on his trousers, he appeared nervous and uneasy. Asking on a couple of occasions whether the police ever passed in this direction.

Parker was seen later the same day talking with man called David Dilcock in a village in the same neighbourhood. Apparently according to Mr. Dilcock, Parker had tried to sell the watch to him, but he refused to purchase it. Parker then hid the watch in a hedge where he could retrieve it later. The next day Parker bumped into William Dilcock, David's brother, he offered the hidden watch to him, but he refused to have anything to do with it.

The police were investigating the murder and had traced Driscoll's movements from the previous day; Parker was wanted for questioning and was eventually arrested and charged with murder.

Mr. Thompson and Mr. Peel prosecuted the case in front of Mr. Justice Smith. Mr. Waddy defended the prisoner. The evidence was circumstantial. Nobody had witnessed the murder, and nobody could place Parker at the scene of the murder. However Parker had not given a statement as to how he attained the property which had been stolen from Daniel Driscoll.

David Dilcock was called to give evidence, about the watch Parker had offered him. Even though the watch had been recovered from the place where Dilcock said it was. His evidence was contradicted. He had given evidence at the Coroner's court; Parker had given him the 4 sovereigns, which he then had spent. In the Crown court he denied having been given any money. The defence picked up on this contradiction, it proved that Dilcock had lied at the Coroner's court, or was lying now.

Mr. Waddy said that, "If Dilcock had told the truth, it might have disclosed the facts as the how the property had been in Parker's possession." He also urged the jury, that if Parker was the person who had committed the offence maybe it was in self-defence, or upon some sudden provocation of the deceased, this would then reduce the crime to manslaughter.

His lordship Mr. Justice Smith in summing up the case directed the jury in that, "Although Dilcock's evidence seemed to be utterly untrustworthy, they would have to consider whether the other evidence in the case was not sufficient to enable them to come to a satisfactory conclusion. There was no evidence which would enable the jury, if they thought the prisoner had killed the deceased, to reduce the crime to manslaughter."

The jury retired, coming back into the court half an hour later, finding the defendant guilty of murder. The death sentence was passed in the usual way.

On the night of the 3rd April 1868, Parker retired to bed at 9.45pm; he slept soundly and was awoken at 5.45 am the next morning. He dressed and prayed for a quarter of an hour, he was resigned to his fate and asked for forgiveness.

At 8am he joined in the service at the prison chapel before going back to the condemned cell.

At 11.30am he fell to his knees and prayed out loud, before Thomas Askern led him to the pinioning room. He walked firmly, calling for Jesus to have mercy on his soul. While he was been pinioned, he continued in prayer.

He handed a letter to the prison governor before being led to the gallows. The letter, addressed to his friends, called upon them to benefit from his fate and warned them against drink, which he said was the cause of him being in the position he found himself in now.

At the gallows outside the York castle jail in front of a huge crowd, that had turned up to witness the execution, Parker shook hands with the governor and other officials. He knelt down in prayer with the prison chaplain before standing; Askern adjusted the noose, Parker shouted, "Lord Jesus receive my spirit." The bolt was pulled and Parker was executed.

Frederick Parker, before his execution asked to see Captain Lawrie the governor, and the chaplain of the prison, he made a signed statement to the effect that he was guilty of the murder and that his sentence was a just one.

This was to be the last public hanging to be performed in public at York. As in May 1868 an act of parliament was passed outlawing public executions, all further executions had to be within the prison walls.

Chapter 4 – The Little Sister

Former Soldier 29 year old William Jackson had served in the 77th Regiment from 1866 until 1872, and then from 1872 to 1874 in the Reserves. Throughout his Army career he served in India until 1870, then went onto Portsmouth. In 1872 he was stationed at both Aldershot, then Chatham, he was discharged in April 1874. Then he returned to live at his parents home at Carthorp, in the West Riding, what is now known as West Yorkshire.

The family home was a little crowded not only did both parents reside there, Jackson's 16-year-old sister and 12-year-old brother also lived there. Therefore Mr. Jackson senior allowed his eldest son to stay provided he slept on the sofa, and abided by 3 simple house rules. There was to be no trouble brought to the door, no drinking, and no swearing. He didn't want his two younger children to get into any bad habits.

Late afternoon of the 4th May 1874, Jackson arrived home at about 6.30pm; he had been drinking all day, and was quite intoxicated. Mr. Jackson senior was livid; a quarrel took place between the two men, the eldest saying, "If you intend on carrying on like this, then you'd better be off. I will not have a drunken man here upsetting the rest of the family."

William Jackson just stood and looked, he remained silent and seemed distracted, then in a rage he picked up a buffet, and threw it towards his father. Fortunately the buffet missed its intended target falling on to the kitchen floor and smashing.

Mr. Jackson senior said to him. "If you do not stop it, I shall go and fetch the police to you."

William replied. "If you do then there will be bloodshed."

Not wanting anymore trouble, Mr. Jackson senior, went upstairs to bed leaving his son to sleep it off on the sofa. Through the course of that night, both parents could hear Jackson, downstairs in which what later described as him being in a deep conversation with himself.

Early the next morning Mr. Jackson set off the work, leaving his son on the sofa sound asleep, he told his wife that he would deal with him when he got back from work that evening.

Jackson later awoke, got dressed, said to his mother that he was going to Bedale, left the house and then walked in the direction of Bedale. Returning home in the early afternoon, again smelling strongly of beer. He packed up his clothes, said to his mother that he was leaving and going to find work in Ripon, he then left.

Five minutes earlier, Elizabeth, Jackson's sister, had started off towards Kirkington. Taking some shoes to a Mrs. Husthwaite, this was in the same direction of Ripon. Jackson quickly caught up with his sister and they walked together for a while.

When they passed the house of Mrs. Johnstone, Jackson insisted that he wanted to call in and say goodbye to her, she was a good neighbour. She had always been kind to him.

Jackson told Mrs. Johnstone that he was going to Ripon, he had heard that a job was going that paid 28 shillings a week, although he would have be happy with 18 shillings.

He went on to say that, "There had been a couple of bad rows at home and he would have one more to finish it."

Mrs. Johnstone said, "It's about time you stopped having rows and be steady, you hit someone at home last night with the buffet."

Jackson replied, "I threw it at my father but it missed. You know, half of these murders that happen are caused by people aggravating a young man when he has had a drink."

Elizabeth then tapped on the window, insisting that they carried on walking. It was 5pm and she wanted to get back home before dark.

They then arrived at Mrs. Husthwaite's home where Elizabeth was to drop of the shoes. Jackson and Mrs. Husthwaite chatted for a while about the army, then left the house. They walked back towards the crossroads where Jackson had to go in one direction and Elizabeth in the other. John Wells and another man were walking towards them, they both noticed that Elizabeth seemed to be upset. They carried on walking and lost sight of them a couple of minutes later.

The next morning around 5am, the dead body of Elizabeth Jackson was found in the field close to where she was last seen. Her throat had been slit from ear to ear. In Elizabeth's pocket was a letter sent from Edwin Gatterley, Elizabeth's sweetheart. It said, ' I have found someone else whom I want to be with more than you, please forgive me for doing this to you.'

Also in the letter was a poem:

I heard the voice of Jesus say come unto me and rest,
Lay down thou weary one,
Lay down thy head upon my breast.

The police initially thought that the course of death was suicide, until they found on a nearby gate post puddles of blood. A doctor deduced that the wound was so severe that she couldn't possibly have done it herself at the gate, then walked the distance to where the body was found.

William Jackson carried on as normal, on the day of the discovery of the body, he was seen at a blacksmith's shop. A day later he pawned his coat and waistcoat, then went to a publichouse ran by a Mrs. Storey in Walworth, on the outskirts of Darlington. He ordered a drink, and then started chatting to the woman whom he had never set eyes on before.

He said to her that. "His sister was being buried the next day, his brother had murdered her and had fled to America where they would not find him. They did not know why his brother had killed her, she was seeing a young man perhaps he was against her seeing him."

Mrs. Storey replied, "It was a bad thing, your brother would be found, he was a villain and he would hang for it." Adding, "Why are you here and not at home with your family and going to the funeral?"

"I called at home yesterday and saw the poor girl, her lips where black and she was snowy white. I loved my sister and could not stay for the funeral. I wish I could get hold of my brother, but he gone to America and will never be seen again."

In the meantime, Edwin Gatterley had been arrested under suspicion of murder and taken to the police station for questioning.

The police conducted a search of the area where the body was found. They discovered near a stream, a pipe, which had a small amount of blood on it and also a razor case.

These items were later shown to the parents of Elizabeth, who were horrified, they identified the items as being the property of William their eldest son.

The hunt for William Jackson then started, a constable walking the streets near Bishop Auckland, spotted a man fitting Jackson's description walking towards him. The man having noticed the constable turned and fled. He was soon apprehended, and taken to the police station at Northallerton.

Jackson was charged with the murder of his sister and remanded in custody. Edwin Gatterley was released without charge.

Jackson while in custody attempted to take his own life, this was unsuccessful and he appeared at the York Assizes in August 1874.

Mr. Price and Mr. Whitacre appeared for the prosecution, Mr. Ethrington Smith at the request of Mr. Justice Denman, defended the prisoner.

The prosecution called as witnesses, the people who had seen Elizabeth in Jackson's company the evening she died. The landlady Mrs. Storey was called to give evidence, as well as the two gentlemen who were the last people to see Elizabeth alive. Jackson's father in his evidence to the court said, "While in the Army, William had received a severe blow to the head. During his last stay at home, he had changed, and seemed crazy at times, repeating the same tale frequently but giving different versions of it. Making his mind up at night to leave home, but the next morning forgetting all about it. Also he had started drinking heavy and would lose his temper often over the smallest of things. He and Elizabeth were very close to each other and she looked up to him."

Private William Smith from the 77th Regiment was called to give evidence, when the defence cross-examined him; he said, "Throughout the time we served in India, William was an inoffensive and quiet man, we returned to England and was stationed at Portsmouth. William got himself into a fight and received a severe blow to the head; this confined him to the hospital, then he seemed to change. He would get quarrelsome after drinking and often would kick his clothes around the room then put them on the fire. I asked him on one occasion why he did these things; he said his head was so bad. He never did anything like this before the blow to his head."

He continued, "We later went to Weymouth were William received another bad blow to his head, from then onwards even a couple of drinks would make him angry and irrational."

The prosecution called the surgeon of the jail to the stand, "In my opinion." He said. "Jackson was sane at the present time."

The prosecution's case was circumstantial; they had placed Jackson near the scene of the crime in the company of the deceased. They found bloodstained property belonging to the prisoner at the scene. Also a witness, who had testified that Jackson, had known about the murder of his sister, even though Jackson had not had any contact with his family since leaving home that fateful day.

The defence urged that the evidence showed that there was great affection between the prisoner and his sister. The entire absence of any motive and the unnatural nature of the crime clearly pointed to the insanity of the prisoner. This theory was undoubtedly supported by the evidence, which, Private Smith and the prisoner's father had given. Both had described the difference between the conduct of the prisoner before and after he had received blows to his head. Mr. Waddy went on to say. "The prisoner since his arrest and his incarceration has strongly denied the allegation and has protested his innocence both verbally to all around him and in letters to family and friends."

The judge summed up the case for the jury, they retired to deliberate and consider their verdict. After been away for only 10 minutes they returned to the court and found the prisoner guilty of murder.

His lordship passed the sentence of death in the usual way. The prisoner was then taken to York castle jail and placed in the condemned cell to wait the execution.

On the Monday before the execution, Jackson attended the Divine service in the prison chapel conducted by the High Sheriff's chaplain, the Hon. Rev. Glyn. After the service, both Reverend Glyn and the prison chaplain the Reverend Thompson escorted Jackson back to his cell. This was at Jackson's own request; they stayed with him for 2 hours. Throughout this time Jackson had maintained his innocence and complained that he hadn't received a fair trial.

The same evening he wrote to his mother and father, sending his love to them and the family. He carefully copied down the whole of 51st Psalm, and begged them to read this in remembrance of him. However this letter did not once contain any denial of his guilt.

Jackson rang the bell of the cell at 1am the next morning, the morning of his execution. He demanded to speak to the governor of the jail Captain Lowrie. He was sent for and attended the cell as the law directed.

Jackson said at once. "I am guilty of murdering my sister."

He then told the governor what really happened that tragic night: When we left Mrs. Husthwaite's I told my sister to go back home. She refused and wanted to walk with me a little further. We carried on for a while, and then she said she wanted to go all the way with me.

I said, "No Lizzie you must go home." She wouldn't go.

She screamed and said, "When you go away you will never write no more."

I said, "I would write."

She said, "No I will come with you, I know what you are like when you go away."

I said, "You cannot come Lizze."

She said, "I want to come and I am coming with you!"

I said, "Goodnight Lizzie." She started to cry.

I shook hands to part with her, turned and walked away.

She chased after me.

I told her to go back but she wouldn't, she wanted to come with me wherever I went.

So I made no more to do, I opened my bag, took out my razor and cut my sister's throat.

She screamed out, blood was rushing from her throat.

She dropped to the floor and I picked her up to move her, she moaned 'OH WILL'.

I laid her in the field, hid my pipe and razor case and disappeared in to the night.

Jackson finished by saying, "I am very sorry for what I have done. I cannot express the remorse like I would like. I loved her more dearly than myself and I hope that God will forgive me. I am sorry for not confessing this great sin before now." Jackson had also written the confession down, he signed it and gave it to the governor.

Later that morning, Thomas Askern came into Jackson's cell. Jackson was waiting for him in a solemn demeanour. Askern pinioned him and then the procession than started towards the 'Drop'.

The church bells could be heard ringing in the distance, the chaplain recited verses from the bible. Jackson walked with a firm step; he was clearly pale, though expressionless. The steps leading to the gallows were wet; Jackson climbed them with ease, then knelt down audibly reciting the Lord's prayer along with the chaplain.

Askern placed the hood over his face, Jackson cried out, "Lord have mercy on me!"

In an instant the bolt was drawn and Jackson plummeted downwards, struggling for 3 minutes for breath, then finally the twitching of the nerves and the muscle spasms stopped. William Jackson was then pronounced dead.

Jackson's execution, was the first execution to be carried out in private, inside the walls of York castle jail. The previous executions had been carried out behind the jail in public. This was deemed to be barbaric, and the law was changed in 1864, outlawing public executions.

Chapter 5 - Sheffield Knife Maker

William Smedley aged 55, was a Sheffield knife-maker, who had been widowed for several years. He had started living with Elizabeth Firth, also a widow with a family, as man and wife. But because of his poor eyesight, it was nearly impossible for Smedley to continue to follow his trade. This brought poverty to the household; therefore Elizabeth in August 1875 told him that she didn't want to live with him under these circumstances. She found new accommodation and moved out.

On the 27th August 1875, John Firth, Elizabeth's son came home from work around 8pm. Smedley and his mum were in the house talking quite friendly. At 8.50pm Elizabeth said to John that they were going out for a while but she wouldn't be long.

The couple walked down to the Harrow Inn public house had a few drinks, and then as it was closing time, they left. Smedley offered to walk her back home.

They were then seen walking down Orchard Street, Sheffield, where Elizabeth was heard to say "No." And then. "No never." Probably this was in reply to Smedley's request to come back to the house with Elizabeth.

When they had reached the doorway of Elizabeth's house, Smedley in a jealous rage grabbed her by the hair, drew his razor and slit her throat. He then turned on his heels and ran away.

Mrs. Nulton, a neighbour observed Elizabeth turn round and then collapse on the front step. She rushed round with another neighbour to help Mrs. Firth, but she was dead, having her throat severely cut, her head nearly decapitated.

Within the hour Smedley went to the town hall police station and spoke to the inspector on duty saying. "I have come to give myself up for murdering a woman named Elizabeth Firth. I have been cohabiting with her, and I have cut her throat with a razor outside her home in Orchard Street; I have thrown away the razor on some slates near the factory by the Iron Bridge. I did not do it because I hated her I did it because I loved her."

He was immediately arrested and a search was performed to locate the razor, this was found in the exact place, which Smedley had described it to be.

At the trial Smedley and his defence council Mr. Gatty, suggested that he did not know what he was doing when he murdered Elizabeth Firth, strongly suggesting the act was the result of homicidal mania.

The prosecution Mr. H. Cadman and Mr. Barker, called the prison governor and the prison surgeon as witnesses and they both gave evidence that they had not observed anything in the prisoner's demeanour to warrant the suggestion that Smedley was insane.

Arthur Hallam the surgeon, who had performed the post mortem, gave medical evidence that Elizabeth's throat had been cut so severely it had cut into her spinal column. The cause of death was recorded as blood loss.

The judge summed the case up to the jury and then said, "The evidence is undisputed nobody saw the incident as it happened, was he or was he not guilty of the crime – unquestionably the answer is yes."

The jury agreed with the prosecution and found that William Smedley was guilty of the murder of Elizabeth Firth.

Before passing sentence the judge asked Smedley if he had anything to say?

Smedley replied, "Nothing that I haven't already said."

The judge before passing sentence said, "You have been convicted by the jury of the wilful murder of Elizabeth Firth. I for one am bound to say that I think no 12 reasonable men would come to any other conclusion than they did. I mean to say there is really no evidence to support your allegation or to show that you are insane." He then went on and passed the death sentence in the usual way.

Thomas Askern executed Smedley at Armley gaol on the 21st December 1875.

Right up to his last breath Smedley was obedient and remorseful, when the white cap was placed over his head, religious passages were heard been spoken by Smedley.

Chapter 6 - Unforgettable Christmas

Boxing Day 1876, John Henry Johnson aged 37 along with his girlfriend Amelia Sewell, and his friend Amos Waite had been drinking all day in the Bedford Arms public house, Wakefield Road, Bradford. The more that was drunk the more they became rowdy and argumentative.

Amelia was walking to the toilet, which was located outside in a small yard, when a few men including a man called Smith and Amos Waite approached her and playfully challenged her.

She screamed out loud for Johnson to come and help. He came to her immediate assistance, grabbing hold of Mr. Smith. In the yard the two men had a scuffle and a couple of punches where thrown. Amos Waite took hold of Johnson and dragged him back into the pub. He said, "It was not Smith that did it, it was me."

Johnson was livid and a quarrel started between himself and Waite. The landlord threw Johnson out in to the street, shortly followed by Amos Waite. A fight then started between the two men, however bystanders managed to separate them both. Johnson was so drunk that a couple of the bystanders managed to take him home and settle him down.

The bystanders left leaving Johnson at home, all most straight away he rummaged through the drawers, until he found the revolver that he had purchased a few years ago while he was in the United States. Taking the revolver he set off back towards the public house. He passed Mr. Smith on the way and threatened him that he was a dead man, then continued back towards the Bedford Arms.

Amos Waite in the meantime had walked home, got changed out of his best clothes, which he had worn all day into his working clothes, before setting off back down to the pub. His wife was anxious about the condition he appeared to be in, worried that he might get into more trouble she followed him.

Waite heard steps following him the street, he turned round and found that his wife was behind him. He shouted at her to go back home. Johnson then appeared out of the shadow's, he pulled the revolver out of his pocket, prodded Amos in the chest with it, then said. "Now then Amos." He then fired the revolver.

The force of the bullet spun Amos around, then sent him crashing to the floor. His wife immediately came to his assistance; blood was pouring out of his chest. Amos laying in agony said, "Oh lass he has shot me!" She screamed for the police but she could do nothing to help Amos, she watched him as he died in her arms.

Johnson, who had already walked half way down the street by the time he heard the scream, he then broke into a sprint, heading away from the Bedford Arms and towards his house. Some of the customers from the public house had heard the shooting and they gave chase. Johnson was eventually caught and held until the police arrived.

He was arrested then searched. Found upon his person was a 7-chambered revolver, which had one chamber spent. He was charged with the murder of Amos Waite and appeared for trial at the Leeds Assizes before Mr. Justice Lopes.

Mr. Whittaker and Mr. Thomas appeared for the prosecution, the prisoner being defended by Mr. Lockwood.

Mr. Whittaker relied on a two handed defence, the first being provocation, which would reduce the crime to manslaughter and the other being insanity, which would get the prisoner off the crime completely.

He submitted evidence to the court that the deceased had been the instigator from the offset, any anger that Johnson had shown, was towards Smith and not the deceased, whom Johnson had always been on the best of terms with.

With regard to insanity, he called evidence from expert witnesses that proved the prisoner's grandfather had died in a lunatic asylum. The prisoner himself from his childhood had shown symptoms of unstableness, desperation, depression and uncontrollable outbursts of temper. More importantly, he had symptoms similar to those his grandfather had been diagnosed of having.

His learned judge in summing up advised the jury, on one hand to give the prisoner the benefit of any doubt, which they may have in their minds. But on the other hand they must firmly, fearlessly and impartially perform their duty if the case was conclusively proved against the prisoner.

He added regarding the evidence, if the interval between the quarrel and the murder which, in this case was 45 minutes, was sufficient enough time to allow the temper to cool and reasoning of the mind to take over, then the prisoner is guilty of murder. But if a sufficient time did not elapse for this purpose, then prisoner is guilty of manslaughter.

With respect of the insanity plea he advised that, if the prisoner at the time of the shooting, knew the nature of the act and the consequences then he should be held responsible, but otherwise he should be acquitted. Mere passion was not insanity, and drunkenness that produces an acquired madness, is not an excuse for committing a crime.

The jury retired to consider the verdict. A short time later they returned, the judge asked the jury if they had come to a verdict and the spokesman replied, "Yes my lord, guilty of murder." The death sentence was passed and the prisoner was taken away to the condemned cell at Armley gaol to await the executioner.

Thomas Askern arrived the afternoon of the 2nd April. He proceeded to make the normal preparations for the hanging, and went through all the correct procedures on the day of the execution.

The prisoner was brought to the gallows, alongside him was the chaplain Rev. Osmond Cookson. He stayed at Johnson's side throughout the pinioning. As the hood was placed over the head of Johnson, the prisoner was heard to say, "Tell my mother I die happy."

However when Askern pulled the lever to open the trap door, the rope snapped and Johnson plummeted through the trap, onto the floor below. The chaplain reacted quickly he called out, "Let us pray for him." Then he jumped through the trap to assist Johnson, who was laid groaning on the ground below. The warders rushed down the steps and brought a chair for him to be seated. The hood and pinions were removed and the chaplain prayed for his forgiveness.

In the meantime a search had been made for a new rope, Askern was busy rigging it up and resetting the trap ready to complete the job, which he had badly botched. Johnson again was made to walk up the 14 steps to the gallows, which he did with dignity. He was pinioned, even with the white hood placed over his head he still could be heard in prayer. Askern pulled the lever and he fell.

Askern had made another mistake, the rope was far too short, and Johnson's neck had not broken. He struggled gasping for breath for 4 minutes, before eventually being pronounced dead.

Outside the gaol nearly 200 people congregated to see the black flag being raised to show that the execution had been completed. Of course they had no idea as to why the delay, or the horrible scene that had taken place within the confines of the prison. A post mortem was later conducted on the body, the cause of death was formally recorded as asphyxia, but no mention about the botched first attempt was made.

Johnson died admitting the justice of his sentence. On the Sunday before his execution he had written a letter to Amos Waite's widow saying, "You know that I would not have done such an awful deed if I had been sober. If the prayers of the living availed at all for the departed, may poor Amos's soul rest in heaven where I hope to meet him. May God bless you and his poor mother and comfort you, this is the sincere wish and prayer of, I may almost say, of a dying man."

This was to be Askern's last execution at Armley goal.

Chapter 7 – The Ships Carpenter

Vincent Walker a 48 year old married man with children was a ship's carpenter. He and his wife were having marriage troubles, his drinking and bad temper normally getting the better of him. Arguments were a constant occurrence at the family home.

Mrs. Walker, after an attack on her, sought justice with the courts. Walker was arrested and charged, at his hearing at the magistrates, he pleaded guilty and was released on a good behaviour bond. If he were involved in anymore disturbances involving his wife, he would be committed to prison.

Mrs. Walker simply couldn't take anymore trouble from Vincent Walker, so she arranged to go and stay with a friend in another part of Hull, there she could consider her options. Also giving Walker time to sort himself out.

She packed her belongings, left the children to stay in the family home with their father, and moved in with her friend. Her friend a master mariners wife, Mrs. Lydia White lived at 37 Nile Street, Hull.

Walker wasn't happy about the arrangement but he couldn't go and complain as he was under bond to keep the peace. All that he could do was hope that she would come back home.

He continued drinking around the pubs in Hull, coming home at all hours drunk. Rumours started circulating that Mrs. Walker was keeping company with other gentlemen. This didn't help Walker, it just prayed on his mind all the time. It seemed that everywhere he went someone would comment about the situation with this wife, and her alleged affairs.

One night in early February 1878, he had been drinking heavily in the public house when someone mentioned to him about his wife and her alleged affair. In a rage Walker pulled an axe out, then announced that he was going round to sort her out. Luckily two customers managed to take the axe from him and calm him down. Two days later he banished a sword again in the local pub-

The crimes behind the hangings

lic house and said that he was going to kill his wife and also Lydia White, for a encouraging her and allowing it to happen in her house. He was eventually disarmed and taken home.

On Sunday 18th February 1878, Walker sent a note to the house of Lydia White, hand delivered by his eldest daughter, nobody was in at Nile Street. Maria, his daughter, gave the note back to Walker.

He was clearly upset, wondering where his wife was and what she was up to, and with whom. He had a couple of drinks, then sent his younger daughter to the house to see her mum. Alice, 16, came back and said she didn't see her, but Lydia had said, that mum was out with two men.

Walker was distraught; he went down to the public house and had a few more drinks. Then he went for a walk around Hull to get his thoughts together. At one point he even broke down and cried. He picked himself up and set of to find some cockles, he knew she loved cockles.

He then set off to the house of Lydia. He walked down her street, carrying a bag of cockles in one hand and a red handkerchief in the other. He knocked on the door and waited. Lydia came to the door and was un-moved to see him stood there. Walker asked if he could speak to his wife, Lydia said that she was upstairs with someone. At this Walker saw red, pulled a knife that was concealed in the handkerchief and attacked her. Stabbing her 30 times on the doorstep.

Mrs. Walker heard the noise in the hallway and come to investigate when she saw her husband stabbing Lydia, she made a dash for the backdoor and ran out of it. Walker saw his wife disappearing into the distance; he didn't have any idea which way that she went, so he thought it would be best to leave it for another day. Walker left Lydia dead on the doorstep and walked off down the street.

Not long afterwards he was apprehended by the local police. He was taken back to the house where the murder was committed.

Lydia was laid on the floor, as the police took him past the body, he kicked out at the corpse. The police dragged him into the kitchen out of the way. When he was asked the reason why he had committed the murder, he said that, "Mrs. White encouraged the wife to sleep with other men. She had even allowed it to happen in her house." Adding, "It was a good job, the wife had run off out of the back door, as she was going to be next."

He was charged with the murder and remanded to appear at the Assizes in York. Mr. Campbell Foster and Mr. Lawrence Gane prosecuted Walker in front of Mr. Justice Pollock. Mr. Lockwood defended the prisoner.

The defence urged the jury to find the prisoner guilty of manslaughter. He had been provoked into the crime by his wife's infidelity. The jury however, after only 20 minutes of deliberation, returned the verdict of guilty of wilful murder.

The learned judge said before passing sentence, "You have been found guilty, after a patient and careful enquiry. I think, there will be no doubt in the mind of any person being present in the court, as to the accuracy of this verdict." He then passed the death sentence in the usual way.

On the Sunday night before his execution Walker wrote a letter to his wife and family, expressing that they take this as a warning to avoid drink. He also acknowledged the justice of his sentence to the governor before he was led to the gallows.

A Roman Catholic priest led the possession, reading the service as he went. Walker when he reached the platform behind within the walls of York castle jail, knelt down and prayed.

He was ready to meet his fate, and was doing so in great firmness. William Marwood placed the hood over his head, tightened the noose, and then pulled the trap to release the trap.

Walker fell. Not enough though to break his neck, he was left writhing in agony for 3 or 4 minutes, slowly dying of strangulation.

Chapter 8 – Master Of Disguise

Charles Frederick Peace was born in 1832 in Sheffield; he was a brilliant musician, inventor, womaniser, prolific burglar, master of disguise, quick thinker, lively and a jovial fellow. But more importantly Charlie Peace was a murderer.

Charles Peace married a widow in 1859. She was called Hannah Ward and she had a young child. Just after the marriage Peace was sentenced to 6 years in prison at Manchester court for burglary, he was released in 1866. Immediately on being released he carried on his trade as a burglar.

He was caught again in 1866 and sentenced this time to 10 years in prison. While serving this sentence, he got caught up in trouble at the jail. He was flogged and transported to Gibraltar. Then was released after serving only 6 years of the sentence.

This prison sentence seemed to have the desired effect on Peace; he went to live with his wife and child in Sheffield. He settled down, even sending his stepson and his own daughter to Sunday school every week. Over the next few years Charlie managed to stay out of trouble.

He started a small business framing pictures, it turned out that he was quite good at this trade, he was soon earning a respectable living. Around this time Charlie lost a finger on one hand, in a pistol accident, and restricting the use of two more. It is not clear as to how this happened, but it is rumoured to by his own pistol going of unintentionally.

Then in 1875 the family moved to Darnell, an area about 5 miles from Sheffield. Continuing to run the picture framing business the family lived quite well.

He was quite a celebrity in his new neighbourhood, with his collection of exotic birds, rare musical instruments and other curiosities that he was only delighted to show to people.

Two doors away lived a Mr. Arthur Dyson a civil engineer and his wife Catherine. Charlie instantly took a shining to Mrs. Dyson and it wasn't long before he befriended Arthur, and was soon a regular visitor to the Dyson's home.

On one occasion he framed a picture of Mr. Dyson's mother, just as an excuse to the visit the house. His picture framing business was booming, so much so that he purchased a Café in Hull, his family moved there, but Charlie stayed mostly in Sheffield to continue running his business.

Charlie then turned his attention to Mrs. Dyson, he took her to music halls, the fair and to the local public house, the couple even had photographs taken together. Charlie even allowed Catherine to charge drinks to his account at the Stag Hotel, near Darnell, when he was not there. The affair was in full swing, Charlie even tried to persuade Catherine to leave her husband and run away to Manchester where he would treat her like a lady.

Arthur Dyson was starting to get suspicious, and aggravated at Charlie always being round at their home. It seemed to Arthur that Charlie was prying into his family's personal affairs. He decided that he didn't want Peace coming around anymore. On the back of a business card he wrote, 'Charles Peace is requested not to interfere with my family.' He threw the card into Charlie's garden that was only two doors away.

This worked for a while or so he thought, but the couple enticed the milkman of all people, to pass hand written notes between the couple. They would often meet away from the house at various places. Mr. Dyson then moved his family away from Darnell on October 29th, to another suburb in Sheffield not telling anyone where they were going.

One of the first people that Mrs. Dyson met at her new home in Banner Cross, was Charles Peace. He went up to her and said, "I am here to annoy you, I will annoy you wherever you go."

Not long after as Charlie was walking down the street with a friend, Arthur Dyson came into view. Charlie pulled out his revolver and said to this friend, "If he offers to come near me, I will make him stand back!" Dyson couldn't believe what he saw, he went to the police station and a summons was issued for Charlie to appear in court.

The date for the hearing coincided with something even more important that Charlie must do. He needed to be in Manchester for another court case that he must attend. The trial of two brothers who were accused of the murder of a policeman called Cock. So he took himself of to Manchester to watch the trial. He sat quietly throughout the proceedings, taking in all what was happening. As soon as William Habron was sentenced to death, Charlie boarded a train and headed back to Sheffield.

The afternoon after he had returned to Sheffield, he went to a public house in Ecclesall, where he entertained the customers by making music from a poker hanging from piece of string, by hitting it with a short stick. He left the public house and made his way to Banner cross, the new home of the Dyson's.

Charles went round the back of the house and stood on a small wall. He could see Catherine in the upstairs back bedroom putting her son to bed, so he whistled the signal that the couple had used many times before. Catherine left the bedroom, walked down the stairs and into the kitchen.

Charlie was watching her every move via the flicking of the candle, which she was carrying. She came outside into the garden and they started talking, shortly afterwards Arthur appeared and made a run at Charlie.

Arthur stood around 6½ foot tall, so Charlie pulled the revolver out of his pocket and fired, purposely missing Arthur. The unperturbed Arthur kept coming at Charlie, he made grab at Charlie, the gun went off and Arthur dropped to the floor, dying.

Catherine rushed to her husband and screamed out, "Murder, you villain! You have shot my husband." Charlie had legged it out of the garden and was stood on the roadside; he hesitated for a moment as what to do next. When he heard the screams of Catherine, he took to his heels and disappeared into the distance, dropping Catherine's letters from his pocket as he fled.

Arriving at a village called Greystones, Charlie disguised his appearance, then grabbed a cab to his mother's house. Having changed and said his goodbyes to his mother and brother, he bought a train ticket to Beverley, boarded the train and left town.

The train arrived at York; Charlie got off and stayed the night out of sight in the station. The next morning he travelled on to Hull hoping to lay low at his wife's café.

Two detectives arrived at the café just as Charlie was about to eat his dinner. They asked Hannah if Charlie was lodging with her. Hannah replied that she had not seen him in a couple of months.

The police were insistent on searching the premises, they were told to go to the side door where they would be let in. This gave Charlie enough time to run upstairs, climb out of a window, onto the roof and hide behind the chimney until they had gone. The police were persistent; they searched the café a few times over the next month, Charlie always being one step ahead of them and concealed himself in various places.

A reward was now being offered of £100 for the capture of Charles Peace. A leaflet was posted in almost every shop window; it contained a detailed description of him, even down to the fact that he had lost a finger.

Charlie had to change his appearance he dyed his hair, shaved his beard. He made a lotion out of walnut shells that he rubbed into his skin to darken it. If that wasn't enough, he managed to get hold of a false arm that he hollowed out, so that it would fit over his own arm. He bought himself a pair of spectacles, and using incredible skill, contorted the features of his face, to totally change his appearance.

Hull was getting a little too dangerous for him, leaving his wife and children behind he left. The next few weeks Charlie was con-

The crimes behind the hangings

stantly on the move, visiting Doncaster, London, Bristol, Oxford, Birmingham, Derby and finally, finishing up in early January at Nottingham.

In Nottingham he lodged at a house belonging to a Mrs. Adamson, who also happened to deal in stolen property. Charlie started a relationship in Nottingham, with another lodger Susan Gray. When he first met her, he pulled out his revolver and said that he would shoot her if she didn't become his.

He carried on his burgling career in Nottingham and surrounding areas. He even returned to Hull for a couple of visits with Susan in tow. The police were looking for him everywhere, he was nearly caught a couple of times, the revolver had to brandished to enable his escape.

Deciding that it would be better to move to London, Charlie packed up, along with Susan Gray, now known as Thompson, they left and moved to 25 Stangate Street, Lambeth.

The next two years were really busy for Charlie, he was a dealer of musical instruments by day, and a burglar by night. He even ploughed some money back into the burgling business, to buy a pony and trip, meaning that he could get to and from his jobs quicker and it provided somewhere to keep the tools of his trade.

Leaving Lambeth he moved onto Greenwich, to Crane Court. Before long, they rented two adjoining houses in the same area. Charlie and Susan living in one and after a little gentle persuasion Hannah and his stepson lived in the other.

Greenwich was not suitable for Mrs. Thompson, so again Charlie arranged another move, this time to Peckam, where all the family could live together in one house.

Charlie was now using the name's John Thompson and John Ward. The family, were thought of as respected neighbours, spending money on improvements to the house, furnishing it lavishly, by means of Charlie's night job.

Charlie even managed to find time to work on a couple of inventions with a gentleman called Brion. They invented a revolutionary fireman's helmet, a device for washing railway carriages and discovered the means of raising sunken ships successfully.

"Patent no. 2635. Henry Fersey Brion, 22 Philip Road, Peckham Rye, London, S.E., and John Thompson, 5 East Terrace, Evelina Road, Peckham Rye, London, S.E., for an invention for raising sunken vessels by the displacement of water within the vessels by air and gases."

The police in the North were surprised that they had not managed to the find Charles Peace, the trail had gone cold and the burglaries had ceased. Meanwhile, the police in London were at a loss as to the new spate of burglaries in the area, but they didn't have any clues as to the perpetrator.

Around 2am on October 10th 1878 a man entered a house in St. John's Park, Blackheath, police constable Robinson saw a light come on he called for two colleagues.

Robinson waited in the garden round the back, one constable waited out on the street while the third went to the front door and rung the door bell.

The man jumped out of the dining room window and walked down the path. Seeing that he was been followed by Robinson, he cried, "Keep back or by God I will shoot you." Robinson kept on coming towards him, 3 shots were fired, only just missing his head. He made a dash for the man; another shot rang out narrowly missing again. Robinson punched him, then the fifth and final shot was fired, hitting Robinson in the arm that had been raised above his face.

Robinson fell to the ground, but managed to keep hold of the burglar's leg pulling him to the ground as well. Both men grappled for a while, the other two constables rushed around the side of the house and the man was arrested. He gave his name as John Ward.

The crimes behind the hangings

Word got to Mrs. Thompson and Mrs. Ward that Charlie had been arrested, they started the process of cleaning the house in Peckam of all the stolen property. Taking some to Susan's sister house in Nottingham and some to Peace's daughter's house in Sheffield.

The police questioned both woman, Hannah Peace, was arrested for aiding an abetting and receiving stolen property. But Susan managed to escape arrest, however the name of Charles Peace was given to the police.

John Ward, the name that Charlie had given at the time of his arrest was charged with the attempted murder of police constable Robinson, he was remanded in Newgate Prison, London.

A police constable, who knew Peace well, was dispatched from Sheffield down to Newgate prison to identify Peace. As the prisoners where doing their morning exercise, walking around the yard, the constable said to the governor, "That is Charles Peace I would know him anywhere."

The trial at the Old Bailey in November 19th in front of the judge Sir Henry Hawkins resulted in Charles Peace alias John Ward, being sentenced to life imprisonment. Without delay Peace was then charged with the murder of Arthur Dyson.

A police constable was sent to America to trace Mrs. Dyson and bring her back for the trial. A train took Peace from Pentonville prison on the morning of January 17th 1879, to Sheffield for the hearing.

He was guarded around the clock by a team of wardens; their sole job was to make sure that he did not escape. The hearing was adjourned the prisoner and his minders boarded the train back to London.

January 22nd 1879, the date for the second hearing, they boarded the train again for the journey to Sheffield. Charlie was making a nuisance of himself, every-time the train started to slow down at a station he was insistent on going to the toilet. The guards soon

46

got annoyed so plastic bags were issued to him; these would then be used then thrown out of the window.

As the train slowed down on its approach to Sheffield, Charlie used one of the bags; the window was opened and, as quick as a flash Charlie dived through the open window. A warden managed to grab his left foot, while another one pulled the emergency stop cord in the carriage. Charlie was hanging upside down out of the window constantly kicking out at the warden with his right foot, eventually succeeding in freeing himself; he dropped onto the line below.

The train stopped shortly afterwards, the wardens rushed back down the line to find Charlie unconscious, a deep wound to his scalp, he lay motionless beside the line. Another train stopped to help. The wardens placed Charlie into the guard's van, and the journey continued.

At Sheffield Peace was taken to the police station and was seen by a doctor, who later pronounced him fit to attend the next hearing which was set for January 30th. In his pocket was a note asking to be buried at Darnell.

It was decided that due to the continued press coverage, the public interest that was by now becoming widespread, and the condition of the prisoner, the hearing would be heard in the corridor near to the cells. A table was placed ready, Peace was brought from the cell and the hearing commenced.

The main point of this hearing as far as the defence was concerned, was to get Catherine to admit they had been having an affair, and that she had written the letters which Charlie had dropped. The affair was critical evidence, if she admitted it, they believed Peace wouldn't get the death sentence.

Throughout this hearing Peace made a nuisance of himself, he constantly interrupted the proceedings. At one point he put his feet up on the table, and his hands behind his head. He was ordered to sit properly and take his feet of the desk. He told his solicitor he wasn't doing his job properly, complained he was cold.

He needed a drink, he wanted this witness called etc. Anything he could do to make a nuisance of himself. His own solicitor told him on one occasion quite abruptly, to be quite!

The magistrates found that there was sufficient evidence for Charles Peace to stand trial at the Leeds Assizes for the murder of Dyson. Peace was remanded in custody and taken to Wakefield jail.

A few days later he was moved by cab to Armley jail, this was done in secret. Charlie only finding out 15 minutes before he was to be transferred. It wasn't the most direct route to Leeds either, it went via Wrenthorpe, Kirkhamgate, Tingley, the outskirts of Morley, Beeston, Holbeck and finally onto the prison.

Thousands of people queued up outside the courtrooms at Leeds on February 4th 1879, wanting to see the infamous Charlie Peace. The public gallery in the court was crammed full, people were being admitted on a ticket only basis.

The trail was presided over by Mr. Justice Lopes, Mr. Campbell Foster prosecuted the case, and Mr. Frank Lockwood defended Peace.

Mr. Lockwood in his opening address said, "Never in the course of my experience, and I defy any of my learned friends to quote an experience. Has there been such an attempt made on the part of those who should be most careful of all others to preserve the liberties of their fellow men and to preserve the dignity of the tribunals of justice to determine the guilt of a man."

Peace interrupted, "Hear Hear!"

Mr. Lockwood continued, "For the sake of snatching paltry pence from the public, these persons have wickedly sought to prejudice the prisoners life. There can be no question that if Mr. Peace had chosen, or was in a position to take out proceedings, more than one newspaper would be open to prosecution for contempt of court."

The first witness to be called for the prosecution was Mrs. Dyson. She described what had happened on the night that her husband had met his tragic death. She maintained even in cross-examination, that her husband, although he might have tried to grab Peace, he didn't actually manage to touch him. Arthur had objected to her friendship with Peace, but they were only friends and had not been intimate. She denied writing letters to Peace, even though the defence showed that they had been wrote by her.

Five witnesses gave evidence that Peace was in Banner Cross the night of the murder. Further evidence was given to the threats issued by Peace to Dyson, when the revolver was taken out. Evidence was also shown that the bullet that shot P.C. Robinson came from the gun that shot Mr. Dyson.

Mr. Lockwood in his address to the jury said, "Peace had gone to Banner Cross, to ask Mr. Dyson to withdraw the warrant for pulling a gun on him. He had no intentions whatsoever of killing or even shooting Mr. Dyson. When the prisoner was talking to Mrs. Dyson in the garden, Arthur who stood at 6 feet 6 inches charged at him in frenzy. The prisoner had to defend himself, he fired a warning shot to make Mr. Dyson stop, but he kept coming at him. In the course of the struggle that followed, the revolver accidentally went off. Tragically killing Arthur Dyson."

Mr. Justice Lopes on summing up the evidence in the case, handed the revolver to each of the jurors asking them to take it, feel the weight of it, place their hands on the trigger and decide themselves, whether it was likely to go off accidentally.

He went onto say, "Mr. Lockwood was perfectly justified to try and discredit Mrs. Dyson as to the letters and the alleged affair. But her evidence, which was backed up by other witnesses, did show that the prisoner had made threats to her and her husband. As she was the only other person present at that fate-full night, was her evidence believable?"

"In my opinion," he added, "It was clearly proved that no struggle had taken place before the murder."

The crimes behind the hangings

At this the jury retired to consider their verdict. 10 minutes later they returned and found the prisoner guilty of murder.

The learned judge passed the sentence of death on the prisoner, who accepted his fate with dignity and composure before being led away.

Charlie now had only 21 days left to live. His family visited him on numerous occasions, all except Susan Thompson. Either his family insisted that he should not see her because she had betrayed him, or the police wouldn't allow her to visit. He did though manage to pass written messages to her.

Reverend Littlewood the vicar of Darnell was requested by Charlie to visit him in his cell.

Charlie thanked him for coming and said he wanted to disclose a few matters to him. Rev. Littlewood sat down and listened to what Charlie was telling him.

Firstly he mentioned the case of the shooting of P.C. Cock in Manchester. A young man called William Habron had been sentenced to life imprisonment for the murder. Charlie knew that this man was innocent, as in-fact he himself was in Manchester in 1876. He was the person that had accidentally shot the policeman, "You may think," Charlie said, "I am an hardened wretch for not coming forward sooner, but what person in my position would have done so?" He went into full details of how it had happened.

This admission of guilt was later passed on to the Home Secretary, who when looking into the case, found that Habron was innocent. He was released him from prison and awarded £800 compensation.

Then Peace went onto explain the shooting of Dyson, then P.C. Robinson. Both men he said had been shot accidentally. "I only take the revolver to scare people, never once I have fired directly at anybody. I always aim away from the person; both men had hold of me. I was trying to get away from them; it went off in the course of the struggle. If I had gone to murder Dyson, which I did not, I would have just walked in through the open door and shot him as he sat reading. I find it hard to believe that I am to die for something which I swore that I would never do, that being taking a man's life intentionally." Peace continued saying over and over again that these shootings was accidental. He finished speaking and both men spent around half an hour praying.

The day before the execution, the last time he was allowed to have visitors, Peace uncharacteristically gave way to uncontrollable grief, and had to be led back to his cell. He prayed with the Rev. Cookson, the prison chaplain into the early hours of execution day. Praying for forgiveness and for the relatives of the men whom he had murdered, and lastly for his family. The chaplain left him for a few hours to get some sleep. He awoke at 5.45am, ate a breakfast consisting of toast, bacon and eggs and tea.

The bells of the prison began to toll at 8am the procession began the short walk to the gallows, just outside the prison, but within its walls. First came the governor, then the under sheriff, then the chaplain reading the service out loud. Peace followed looking worn and haggard but much healthier than at his trial. Wardens supported him on both sides.

Peace walked the steps up to the gallows and was met by William Marwood, who pinioned him and put the rope around his neck. Marwood was in the process of putting the hood on Peace when he said, "Don't, I want to look."

The chaplain got to the part of the service where the prisoner could speak, Peace prayed out loud, "God have mercy on me, Lord have mercy on me. Christ have mercy on me." Marwood thinking that he had finished reached over to place the hood on him. Again he was stopped by Peace saying, "Don't, stop a bit, if you please."

He then turned his head towards the reporters addressing them he said, "You gentlemen reporters I wish you to notice the few words I am going to say to you. I know my life has been base and bad. I wish you to ask the world after you have seen my death, what man could die as I die, if he did not die in the fear of the Lord. Tell my friends that I feel sure they have sincerely forgiven me, and that I am going into the Kingdom of Heaven, or else to that place prepared for us to rest in, until the great judgement day. I hope that no person will taunt my children for what I have done. God bless my children, my children, each goodbye. Oh my Lord God, have mercy on me!"

Marwood by this time had had enough; he pulled the hood over Peace's head to shut him up. Peace trying to disrupt the proceedings again said, "I should like a drink, do you have a drink for me?" Marwood ignored his request; the chaplain continued the service while Marwood was adjusting the noose.

Peace again interrupted and said to Marwood, "That's too tight." The chaplain said, "Lord Jesus receive his spirit." Marwood instantly pulled the bolt and Peace fell through the trap, out of view, dying instantly.

The Governor had 16 letters addressed to friends and family of Charles Peace's, that Charlie had written and given him the night before. He was instructed to send them after his execution. Each letter had a card inside reading.

'In Memory of Charles Peace,
who was executed in Armley prison.
Tuesday, February 25th, 1879 aged 47,
For what I done but never intended.

Chapter 9 – Leeds Gamekeeper

Mr. Wheelhouse, Mr. Greenhow and Mr. Lockwood commenced the prosecution case of 22 year old John D'arcy at the May 1879 Spring Assizes in Leeds, before Mr. Justice Manisty. Mr. Blackburn had been instructed to act on behalf of the prisoner.

John D'arcy the defendant was accused of murdering William Metcalfe a 75 year old gamekeeper at this home at Oulton, 6 miles south east from Leeds.

The prosecution stated that, "The evidence that they would show to the court, even though in parts some evidence was circumstantial. It was the full account of the brutal murder of an elderly gentleman. Three men, Mr. Morley, Mr. Batler and Mr. Walker, as well as a Mrs. Jeffrey's will give evidence that they saw a man in the house of Mr. Metcalfe. They had also picked out the man later, at an identity parade. That man is the prisoner."

Mrs. Sarah Jeffrey's was called to the stand. She was a married woman living in the village of Oulton, she said, "I was passing the lodge of Oulton Hall, at 6.45pm on the evening of the 4th March. I heard a scream then a voice saying, don't murder me, don't murder me. I knew it was the voice of Mr. Metcalfe so I walked up with pathway. The door was ajar, and I peered in. I saw the prisoner coming towards me, then the door slammed in my face. I ran to get help, bringing back with me Alfred Morley."

Alfred Morley a gardener said, "I heard a woman scream, then Mrs. Jeffrey's called me over. I went to a window at the south side of the lodge. I saw a man kneeling down with his back towards me, he was wearing a Billycock* hat. I went away and fetched John Walker. We looked through the window again, and saw the same man, trying to unlock the top door of a chest of drawers. I didn't go into the house because I was scared, Walker held the front door and I went and got P.C. Ross."

William Batler a collier said, "I was 50 yards from the lodge gates on that evening, a little before 7pm. I heard a woman scream; I went to see what was happening. I went to the back door, and saw a man coming along the passageway with a weapon in his hand. It looked like a pistol; it seemed to be pointing at me. John Walker was also at the back door, he soon left and went round to the front. The man was wearing a Billycock hat, as well as a coat that I do not remember the colour of. He had a collar and tie on, similar to what the prisoner is wearing now. I went round the front, Walker was holding the front door shut, and Morley had gone for the police. I thought that I would watch the best I could, and went back around the back. When I got there, the back door it was slightly ajar."

John Walker a tailor said, "I looked through the back window and saw a man, then I went round the front and held the door knob. Someone on the inside was turning it, I was scared, I didn't go in, instead I waited until the police came."

Police constable John Ross said, "I first met the prisoner early evening around 5.55pm. He was walking down Woodlesford Lane wearing a felt hat, brown coat and carried a black case. An hour later I was called to the lodge where I found Mr. Metcalfe dying. Other people at the scene described the person they had seen in the house, this matched the man I saw walking in the street an hour earlier. The prisoner had just been released from Jail and was under a 5-year police supervision order, we knew who he was, and where he lived. I boarded the 7.56 train from Woodlesford station to Leeds, where along with Sgt. Lumb we called at a house in Mulberry Street. We got no answer so we waited opposite in the out-house's and waited. At 10.10pm the prisoner walked down the street and went into the house we were watching. After waiting for 5 minutes, we went into the house and arrested D'arcy. Sgt. Lumb said I have come to arrest you for the murder of William Metcalfe. His reply was, Oh lord, am I charged with a serious deed like that? I have been to Bramley (5 miles the other side of Leeds) all day, and I have not been in that lodge for 5 weeks."

Ross went on, "We found the Billycock hat and took him to the police station. The witnesses all recognised him in the identity parade when he was wearing the hat."

Other witnesses were called to give evidence regarding various items of property, which were later found. The poker had been found which now had traces of blood on it, as well as grey hairs from the victim.

A chisel was found, this was proved to be the property of the prisoner. A fellow work mate had given it to him, not long before the murder.

Two police constables said that they found footprints in the soft soil, at the back of the Lodge that matched the boots which D'arcy owned.

Inspector Turton said, "At Wakefield courthouse, I had attempted to put the felt hat on the prisoner so eyewitnesses could identify him. He threw it down saying you have put that on me 3 times now; you better not try again for you own safety. He was very excited and violent. We made him wear the hat, the prisoner said that, you'd better bring the poker which I did it with, put it in my hand, and get them all to look." This evidence was corroborated by another police officer.

Mr. Blackburn on behalf of the prisoner stood and addressed the jury saying that; "I would make a few remarks on the deficiencies in the case for the crown, and then detail shortly afterwards the nature of the case I intend to put in answer. The jury must first of all, remember the evidence laid before them was merely circumstantial. The danger of convicting any man of a capital offence on such evidence would be obvious, even if a recent miscarriage of justice (probably referring to the William Habron case) had not impressed as much on the minds of all".

"Someone most cruelly murdered William Metcalfe, but, was the prisoner the type of man likely to commit such an outrage? Was it not more like the work of a passing tramp unknown to the habitants of Oulton? It was hardly conceivable that a man would leave a meeting of Sunday school delegates, then go and commit a horrific murder. Several of the witnesses must have been mistaken as to the time they said they saw the prisoner on the afternoon of the 4th. He would show without doubt, the prisoner was

The crimes behind the hangings

at Bramley up until dinnertime that day. And at 8.10pm, he was seen in the Crooked Billet public house at a place called Thwaite's Gate, where he then boarded a tram. As for the tailor, the collier and the gardener from Oulton, what did the jury make of their evidence? 3 men who stood by while the murder was being committed, and did not do a thing to help. They could have saved the man from dying, or at least grabbed the intruder. Although they did nothing but stand and watch."

Referring to the evidence of the chisel and boots, he said, "The evidence about the footprints must be regarded almost with contempt. There were no nails or distinctive marks, just a pattern print in the soil, from a pair of boots that are sold each and everyday in Leeds, and possibly every other city in England. The chisel which was found near Metheley, was made by a large manufacturer in Sheffield, it might have been the property of almost any joiner in the country."

Mr. Blackburn called on Michael Armisty. His evidence was that D'arcy was in the Cooked Billet, Hunslet, Leeds, at 8.10pm. He was a tram conductor and D'arcy bought him a drink, then they both boarded the tram to Leeds. The tram driver also gave evidence that D'arcy was on that tram.

Other witness were called and confirmed that D'arcy was seen that day, wearing a coat and a tall hat, and carrying an umbrella. Not one witness said that he was carrying a black case.

On summing up the case to the jury he said, "It was an impossibility that D'arcy could have been at Oulton Lodge at 7pm on the evening of 4th March. The chisel was found near Metheley, which is a few miles west of Oulton. Oulton is south west of Thwaites Gate, it would take at least 2 hours to get from Oulton to Thwaites Gate, and considerably longer to get there from Metheley."

"How could the prisoner have a confirmed sighting at 8.15pm by two men, but also be 8 miles away having just committed a murder? The prisoner is a reformed character since his release from Spikes Island prison, Ireland. He attends the South Accommodation chapel at Hunslet, on Sunday evenings. He is a Sunday school teacher there, and also attends the Roman Catholic chapel on Sunday Mornings. As well as being a delegate of the Leeds Sunday school Union, South Parade Leeds. He was there for a meeting until 5.20pm on the afternoon of the murder. He could not have possibly left that religious meeting, hopped on board a train, be seen at 5.55pm at Woodlesford Lane, near Oulton by P.C Ross. Murdered Mr. Metcalfe at 7pm, and got back to Thwaites Gate by 8.15pm."

His lordship congratulated Mr. Blackburn on his able defence, then directed the jury.

"What occurred on the 4th of March when the prisoner was alleged to be in Oulton. It was only by examining every minute of the journey, could they come to a conclusion. If they suspected that the prisoner was in Oulton that day, they should consider him then going to Oulton lodge. But if they thought that there was sufficient enough evidence to show, that he had boarded the tramcar at 8.15pm that evening, he could not have been at Oulton lodge or indeed anywhere near where the chisel was found. They would have to weigh the relative credibility of witnesses, who professed to have seen the prisoner after the murder at several places, miles apart. There was also the evidence of the footprints; such evidence is sometimes conclusive, other times it is almost useless. The statements that the prisoner had made at the time of his arrest, may, or may not, have influence on the verdict of the case."

The jury found the prisoner guilty of murder. The judge asked D'arcy if he had anything to say before sentence was passed?

He replied, "I am innocently convicted, praise the Lord. I cannot but return thanks to your lordship and the jury for the kindness you have exercised in the examination of the case. I have no doubt that the guilty one will be found out one day. But it will be when it is too late. Into the hands of the Lord I commend my spirit."

Adding, "I only find fault with the untruthful evidence of the police. The jury have given their verdict on the evidence put to the court."

Right up to the moment he was executed D'arcy retained his innocence. He spoke of only the perjury of the police witnesses.

On the morning of the 15th April 1878, he walked with the utmost coolness to the gallows, where William Marwood was waiting for him. Father Fryer asked him if he had anything to say, D'arcy replied, "I am innocent, nevertheless I acknowledge the justice of my sentence, Lord Jesus, receive my soul."

The bolt was drawn at that instant, and the prisoner died without a struggle.

Billycock Hat! Very similar to a bowler hat, it was designed in 1849 by the London hat makers Thomas and William Bowler, and created for the Edward Coke the younger brother of the 2nd Earl of Leicester.

Chapter 10 – The Cracked Watch

The packed court room at York in front of Mr. Justice Stephen, sat waiting for the jury to take their seats, John Henry Wood aged 27 stood patently in the dock, apparently taking last minute instructions from his defence council Mr. Lawrence Gane. Mr. Lockwood, Mr. Fenwick and Mr. Ellis all appeared for the prosecution, and were sat quietly reading their notes.

The jury was seated and the clerk of the court asked the accused to stand. He then said. "John Henry Wood, you have been charged that on or about the 19th February last, that you did wilfully murder John Coe at Rotherham, how do you plead guilty or not guilty?"

The prisoner in a firm and clear voice said. "Not guilty."

Mr. Lockwood then stood up and introduced himself, his colleagues and Mr. Gane to the jury. He went on to say. "It is pointless for me to impress on the you the seriousness of the crime which the prisoner is charged with, I urge you, the jury to give your full attention to the evidence which shall be brought before you. We the prosecution shall show that on the 19th February 1881, Mr. John Coe was attacked with a wooden stake, beaten around the head and body until all life was extinct. He was then robbed of a watch and chain along with a few shillings".

"The badly beaten body was left at the side of the road, in full view of any passers-by. We will show that the prisoner had been in the company of the deceased throughout the evening before he met his death. The prisoner had the motive, was the last person to see the victim alive. When he was arrested he had the victims property, namely a watch and chain in his procession. John Henry Wood, we will show, murdered Mr. Coe in the most despicable, cowardly fashion imaginable."

Mr. Hawksworth was called to the stand, in his evidence he stated that; he was walking to work on the morning of the 19th February 1881, around 6.20am, he was on a road which went from Catcliffe, where he dwelled to Rotherham where he worked. He came across a haystack by the side of the road, laid at the side of the haystack was a body of a man. He did not interfere with the body in anyway, but it was quite obvious that the man was dead. He summoned for a police constable and Sgt. Morley from Rotherham arrived on the scene.

Sergeant Morley was called to the stand and said. "I arrived and saw the body laid at the side of the road blood was everywhere, I felt the body, it still appeared to be warm. Laid next to the body was a branch from a tree, which appeared to have had its bark removed, it was possibly used as some form of walking stick. There were two wounds that were apparent to me, one to the left temple and the other to the forehead. I looked around and found close by a broken stake, the end of which was covered in blood. The body was transported to the dead house (mortuary) and was identified as Mr. John Coe."

The police doctor then gave evidence. "I examined the body shortly after if was discovered, it is my opinion that the body had been dead for between nine and ten hours. The post mortem showed that the death was the result of a depressed fracture of the skull. Which had quite clearly been caused by a blow administered with horrendous violence."

The prosecution then went on to show the movements of John Coe on the day before he met his tragic death. Mr. David Coe, John's uncle was called to give evidence.

He said. "We left John's parents home at Brinsworth, on the morning of the 18th. We went to the dog track and then to the Chequers Inn, which is at Whiston. John was wearing as usual a silver Geneva watch attached to a steel curb chain. Attached to the chain were a watch key and a red seal, mounted in gold metal. The watch glass had a crack in it, but it still kept perfect time. Around 6pm that afternoon, Wood who lived near by came into the public house, John bought a round of drinks, paying for it with half a sovereign, the landlord gave him the change. John always carried a walking stick, which he generally cut from a hedgerow. A man called Willison was also in the pub and he asked John if he would exchange his stick for one with the bark removed, John agreed and the exchange was done. Around 7.15 we left with Chequers Inn along with Wood and went to towards the Belvedere Inn on the road to Rotherham. This is the point where I left the other two, they carried on towards the Butchers Arms."

Mr. Willison was called; he collaborated the evidence regarding the walking stick that David Coe had swapped him.

Mrs. Oates the landlady of the Butchers Arms, confirmed that the two men had been into her public house on the evening in question. They had a couple of drinks, paid for by John Coe and then they both left, going in the direction of the Rotherham.

A Mr. Wright was called he said. "I met the two men in the Pack Horse Inn, they had just arrived from the Butchers arms. They told me they were going on to the Mail Coach Inn next so I tagged along and went with them. Just before last order's was called, John ordered a gallon of ale to take away, he paid of it; he seemed to have been paying for drinks all night. We then left the Mail Coach Inn, along with two girls that John and Wood had been chatting to. I left them, they said that they were going to a local house presumably owned by one of the woman. Wood was walking with a walking stick which Coe had been using earlier."

A cab driver called Mr. Holmes said that. "He was waiting for a fare outside a club on High Street, Rotherham, at around 11.40pm he saw the deceased and the prisoner walking together."

He further said that. "Later that night he saw the same two men walking in the direction of where the body was later to be discovered."

Mr. Lockwood said for the prosecution. "Nothing further was seen of the two men that evening, nor was John Coe ever to be seen alive again. His body was discovered the next morning." He then called to the stand a Mr. Wadsworth.

Wadsworth said. "On the morning of the 19th I was walking away from the village of Whiston towards, what I know now to be the area that John Coe had been found murdered. I saw John Wood walking away from the murder scene and towards me. He stopped and we had a brief conversation, I noticed that he was wearing a silver Geneva watch on a silver curb chain."

The landlord of the Stag Inn, Whiston, said. "Wood came in for a drink on that morning, he appeared to have slept rough. He told me that he was so drunk the previous evening that he could not make it home, so he had slept in a shed belonging to a Mr. Leedham, who lived in the village."

"In which direction is Mr. leedham's house? Is it in the direction of where the body was found?" Asked Mr. Lockwood.

"No sir!" The landlord replied. "It's in the opposite direction." He went on, "Shortly before 11am that morning, someone came in to the bar and said that a body had been found murdered on the road towards Rotherham. Wood made a comment that the murdered man had a relation who had one arm, and was known as Cliff. I thought this was a little strange, no news of the murder victim had been forthcoming, how did Wood know this information"

"Exactly." Exclaimed Mr. Lockwood.

Mr. Poynter gave his account of the morning. "I met up with John Wood on the morning of the 19th February, Wood said that he had plenty of money, and he had a watch which he wanted to sell. He showed me the watch; it was a silver Geneva watch, on a silver curb chain. Attached to the chain were a red seal and a watch key. I said that I would take it and try to sell if for him. I later opened the back of the watch with a knife, and found the inscription 'Needham - Rotherham'. I couldn't sell it, so I gave him it back."

In cross-examination Mr. Gane said. "Was the watch face cracked?"

"I don't remember." Was the reply.

"You don't remember, you took the watch and tried to sell it, now you don't remember."

"No sir, I don't think that it was cracked." Was the reply.

A man called Ellis was the next witness to give evidence, he said, "I came across Wood in Rotherham. I asked him if he heard of the murder that everyone was talking about? He said that he hadn't, so I told him what I had heard. Wood went pale and looked stunned, he said to me that it was John Coe, and that he had been out with him the previous evening."

Mr. Lockwood then carried on. "Wood then disappeared, nobody saw him until he was arrested 9 miles from Whiston on the 27th February. When arrested he remarked, according to the arresting officer, "I know the job, which you want me for, but I have never had a watch in my life. He was charged with murder and remanded in custody."

He was locked up with another prisoner, discussing the case together the other prisoner said. "That watch will do you John."

Then Wood replied. "That's all right, if it all turned against me, it would only be a month for manslaughter."

Mr. Lockwood summed up the case for the prosecution by saying. "I remind the jury that you are only concerned with the facts of the case, with the evidence put before you. The facts have only one conclusion, that was, John Henry Wood was guilty of the murder of the deceased."

Mr. Lawrence Gane addressed the jury on behalf of the prisoner; "There are many facts in this case that could be used for both the defence, and the prosecution. These facts form a tragic and cruel background to a crime that was committed. A crime which my client, Mr. Wood being the central figure. The first thing that must be addressed is the motive; the prisoner had absolutely no motive for taking the life of the victim. They had met that evening as friends, been drinking together as friends. He had not been wronged by, nor, had he wronged the deceased throughout the evening. If the motive, as the prosecution case strongly suggests was robbery, was it not possible that through drink the victim was at the mercy of anyone wanting to rob him, without the need for extreme violence."

"There were many links that the prosecution relied on, the stick being one. Wood was last seen with the stick on that night by the cab driver Mr. Holmes. The stick was later found next to the body of the dead victim." Mr. Gane continued, "Would it not have been appropriate to return the property you had borrowed, before parting and going your separate ways?"

"On hearing that a murder had been committed the prisoner showed no emotion at all. But when he heard the description of the victim, a man whom he had spent the previous evening in the company of, he trembled violently. Were these the actions of a guilty man, or where they the reactions of any ordinary man with human feelings?"

"The missing Geneva watch, which the prosecution had stated was stolen by the perpetrator of the murder. Many jewellers throughout the North of England sell watches identical to Mr. Coe's. A peddler sold the red seal; undoubtedly he sold many others. Mr. Coe's watch according to his uncle had a crack on the glass face. The watch that Wood had, the one he asked Poynter to sell. Did not have a crack on the face. Wasn't it also inconceivable that a murderer would commit a crime, then show the property he had stolen to others, the very same day, and within yards of the spot where the body was found?"

He added. "Many of the statements that have been made in this court room, on behalf of the prosecution are undoubtedly false, they are wild and absurd. No member of the jury should be asked to believe them!"

His lordship addressed the jury in his summing up, said, "They must be satisfied before they could find the prisoner guilty of murder, beyond all reasonable doubt, that the prisoner had murdered the victim. It would not be enough for them to suppose guilt was probable, they must go further and suppose innocence improbable. If the watch given to Poynter, was not the watch that belonged to Coe, why was it that this watch was not produced in evidence, either to prove the watch was Coe's, or, to prove that the watch wasn't, where is the watch now?"

The jury retired to consider their verdict at 1.50pm, they returned to the court at 2.20pm; they found the prisoner guilty of murder.

The judge donned the black cap, looked directly at the prisoner and said, "John Henry Wood, you have been convicted of wilful murder. A wilful murder committed under circumstances of extraordinary atrocity. The jury has listened patiently to the whole of the evidence, and has carefully weighed the arguments of your counsel. They have no doubt as to your guilt, nor have I any doubt. You passed the day with your victim in good fellowship; you went as a friend with him from place to place. You went at last to a place where you thought you could effect your purpose undetected, then struck the man to death with a deadly weapon. For the purpose of obtaining, a few shillings, a watch and chain. For that crime you must die."

He then went on and passed the sentence in the usual way.

Wood was taken away to York castle jail, placed in the condemned cell and waited for the William Marwood to arrive, which he did on the 10th May 1880. Then executed him the next morning.

Chapter 11 – Sheffield Cutler

James Hall, aged 53 worked as a Sheffield Cutler, he lived with his wife Mary Ann Hall and their daughter Selina Hall at Shelf Street, Sheffield.

Hall had led a strange life over the last few years; he would sometimes work for a fortnight or so, then turn to drink for weeks on end. He repeatedly threatened to kill his wife with a hatchet, and had taken his hand to her many occasions, when he was drunk.

On march 26th 1881, Selina come home around 4.30pm and found that both her parents were out. Hall come home soon afterwards, got changed. Then left the house again before Mary came home at 6pm.

James returned at 8.30pm, Mary was not impressed that he had gone out drinking. A blazing argument started between the couple. Selina was upstairs at the time; she could hear the voices but could not tell what was being said.

Mary shouted up to Selina saying, "He said let us live together comfortably, or it will be worse for me." Selina came down the stairs, spoke to her dad, then left the house with her mother at about 9pm.

Selina went for a walk with her boyfriend; a young man named Duckingfield. Mary went to visit a neighbour. She was last seen entering her house, just after 11pm that evening, by a Mr Betts who was walking past at the time.

Selina came back to the family home at 11.30pm, finding the front door locked, she banged on the door. Getting no answer she went round the back of the house to retrieve a spare key for the door. Looking through the kitchen window she saw her father standing over the body of her mother, with a hatchet in his hand.

She rushed back around to the front of the house and was met by Hall, still holding the blood-covered hatchet. He swung the hatchet towards Selina, the force luckily being deflected by the umbrella, which she was carrying; however the hatchet did hit her on the face wounding her.

Selina's boyfriend, Mr. Duckingfield grabbed Hall, and attempted to take the hatchet from him to stop any further attacks. Two men passing by, also came to give assistance and eventually Hall dropped the weapon. The men held onto Hall until the police arrived.

Upon entering the house of Hall's, the police were greeted by a horrific sight. Mary was dead on the floor, her head on the left side, had almost been split in two. Blood was splattered up the walls nearly 4ft high. Police constable Crowe took Hall into custody. When Hall was charged by him, he replied, "I did it and I meant to do it."

Mr. James the police surgeon arrived at the house at 2am, after examining the body, he found several wounds to her head and neck. These wounds were the cause of death and most likely would have been caused by the hatchet the prisoner was carrying.

Hall was charged with the wilful murder of his wife Mary Ann Hall, he was taken before the magistrates court in Sheffield, where he made a statement to the court.

His statement alleged that about three years ago, on coming home one night, he found a man named William Loude in the company of his wife, and that he told his wife then, he would have her life if he ever found her at it again.

He went on to say that, when he came home on the 26th march, he found his wife and a man who he thought was Loude together on his sofa. The man got away, upsetting the kitchen table on his way out. Then in a drunken rage he had picked up the hatchet and attacked his wife. The case was adjourned to the Assizes and Hall was remanded in custody.

The case reopened at the Leeds Assizes before Mr. Justice Kay. Mr. Stuart Wortley and Mr. Charles Ellis appeared for the prosecution, Mr. Vernon Blackburn and Mr. Harper represented the defendant.

The prosecution called William Loude to give evidence. He said that. "I have known James Hall for many years, I have never been to his house, and I definitely have never had any improper relations with Mary Hall."

Selina Hall was called as a witness; her evidence showed that Mary had never had any extra marital relationships with Loude or any other person.

The police stated in evidence that, on examination of the house, the kitchen table was neatly set. Plates with meat and other items were on the table; there was nothing at all to suggest it had been overturned. Nor did the condition of the kitchen corroborate the prisoner's statement.

The defence's closing address to the jury suggested that Hall had been drinking heavily for months before he killed his wife. His mind was so disordered by the suspicions of his wife's infidelity; he in fact had asked his wife on numerous occasions, where she had been and what she had been doing. Even going as far as suggesting to Selina that her mother was doing what she ought not to. At the time he killed his wife he was not responsible for his actions.

The judge in summing up to the jury, pointed out what the law on the subject was, calling for their attention to all the evidence, which had been laid down before them, and asked them to retire and return their verdict. 45 minutes later the jury returned to the court, finding the prisoner guilty of murder.

Mr. Justice Kay passed the death sentence in the usual way and the prisoner was taken away to be executed on the 23rd May 1981 at Armley jail by William Marwood.

Chapter 12 – Rising Sun

The skipper and owner of Hull boat, the Rising Sun, Osmond Otto Brand aged 27, had in April 1881 taken on a young 14 year old apprentice for 7 years. The lad, William Pepper was a small boy and wanted to learn all the aspects of being a fisherman. The Rising Sun left Hull docks just before Christmas 1881, William Pepper would never see dry land again.

The boat returned back from its voyage on the 6th January 1882, arriving at Hull docks, Brand immediately went to the police station, where he saw police constable John Harvey. Brand reported that on the 1st January at 5.30am, William Pepper had been knocked overboard by the big foresail sheet and had tragically drowned.

The police investigated the incident; it came apparent that William Pepper had been cruelly treated on the voyage. He had been badly beaten, starved, stripped naked, and locked up in the hold. They brought Brand and the rest of the crew in for questioning; eventually charging Brand with murder and a crewman called Rycroft with Common assault.

The case was heard at the Assizes in Leeds before Mr. Justice Watkin Williams. Mr. Waddy and Mr. Mellor appeared for the prosecution, Mr. Kershaw and Mr. Fenwick defended Brand and Mr. Lawrence Gain represented Rycroft.

Rycroft pleaded guilty to the charge of common assault, Mr. Gain stood to address his lordship on Rycroft's behalf, as is normal before sentence is passed. Mr. Kershaw, Brand's council, objected by saying, "The learned council could not extenuate Rycroft's offences without making remarks which, would jeopardise the case against my client."

His lordship agreed and stated that; "It would be better for the case against Brand, if this matter was left in my hands." Shortly after he sentenced Rycroft to 3 months hard labour.

The crimes behind the hangings

The case against Brand was then opened; the prosecution called the second mate on board, William John Dench. "We left Hull just before Christmas, shortly after leaving, the skipper said that he would make Pepper pay for telling lies about him."

"What lies?" Asked the prosecution.

"On the dock just before we left, as the skipper was with his wife, Pepper had said that his sister knew him." Adding, "I asked Pepper if he been telling lies and he denied doing so."

"Then what happened."

"The skipper thrashed him repeatedly and threw buckets of water over him, knocked him down, kicked him with his heavy boots, jumped on his stomach and then dragged him around the deck. He made Pepper remain on the deck throughout most of the voyage. He was stripped naked and water was thrown over him.

He was kept without food until he was weak and ill and couldn't speak. This treatment was kept up for days, until the skipper threw him in the hold, which had 3 or 4 foot of water in. He was brought up on deck again, the skipper jumped on him from a height of about 5ft and then kept kicking him. The boy was tied over the side of the boat and left there for hours on end. The skipper hit him between the eyes with his fist and as Pepper laid motionless on the deck; he kept hitting and hitting him. The skipper was told that Pepper was dying, and he replied 'a good job too'.

In fact Pepper did die shortly afterwards and he was thrown overboard naked. The captain always carried a gun, he waved it about telling us all, that we should all stick to the story of the sail hitting Pepper forcing him overboard."

William Blackburn, spare-hand aboard the boat, gave corroborative evidence and also added, "Brand fed Pepper with some bones that the dog had finished with and also some potato skins."

Blackburn was then cross examined and from the evidence he gave it was clear that all crew members of the Rising Sun, except for a man called David Yates, had been involved in the cruelty of William Pepper. They had all gone along with the skipper, agreeing that pepper had fallen over board, in order that Yates would believe this story.

Mr. Waddy summed up the case to the jury saying. "I do not see how it is possible for the jury to escape from the conviction, that the deceased had, by a course of cold blooded, deliberate and persistent injuries, been cruelly murdered by the very man whose duty it was to protect him."

Mr. Kershaw addressed the jury on behalf of the defendant, referring in strong terms to the prejudice against his client that had been created by comments in most of the newspapers. He brought to the attention of the jury, the characters of the witness's that had given evidence against his client; all except one had participated in the cruelty. It also seems apparent that the crew did not regard the prisoner's actions towards the boy, to be very cruel, nor did anyone know that the boy was dying. Finishing the address by saying, "The prisoner had no intention of killing the boy, he did not know until the very last moment that the boy was dying, his crime was not murder but manslaughter."

The learned judge in his summing up to the jury said. "It is necessary in our mercantile marine that captains should be invested with great authority. But it was also essential that judges and juries should step in, for the purpose of seeing that such authority was not abused. If the prisoner, in the exercise of his authority, felt it his duty to punish severely, harshly and continuously, but by an error of judgement inflicted excessive punishment, and so caused death, he would be guilty of manslaughter. It seemed to him that the jury had no alternative than either to acquit the prisoner or find him guilty. If they believed the evidence then they must find him guilty of murder, if they disbelieved the evidence then he should be acquitted."

The jury retired to consider the verdict, and returned to the courtroom 10 minutes later. They found the prisoner guilty of murder.

The judge asked Brand if he had anything to say as to why the death sentence could not be passed, he replied in a firm and clear voice said, "I am not guilty of murder, my lord."

The judge then put on the black cap and addressed the prisoner; "I have never read or heard of a crime of greater atrocity of the one which you have been found guilty by your peers."

He then passed the sentence of death in the usual way.

Brand received his sentence with perfect composure, walking away from the dock without any assistance, the spectators in the court, both men and women hissed and booed him. It took sometime before order was restored. He was taken away to Armley jail and hanged on the 23rd May 1882 by William Marwood.

Chapter 13 – The Gleaner

At the Assizes on the 10th November 1882 Edward Wheatfill aged 33 was charged with the murder of Peter Hughes, on board the Gleaner, a British fishing boat. Mr. Lawrence Gane and Mr. Lockwood conducted the prosecution Mr. Mellor acted for the prisoner.

The case according to Mr. Gane was as such: The Gleaner, a fishing smack left Hull on the 12th January, the crew consisted of Captain Callan, 1st mate Wheatfill, 2nd hand Peaks, a 3rd hand, deckhand Ratzloff and 16 year old Peter Hughes, the ships cook.

Hughes was a strong, healthy, vigorous lad, a little clumsy but with a helpful and willing manner. From the outset Wheatfill began to subject Hughes to the most heartless and brutal cruelty. Making his go on deck in the coldest of weathers completely naked. He was also made to carry a heavy bucket containing gallons of water upon his head.

This treatment went on for days; Hughes dropped the bucket on occasions due to his weakness. He was made to clean up the water refill the bucket, then complete the process over and over again.

Wheatfill lashed Hughes naked to the winch, left him for hours to the mercy of the North Sea elements. Meals were withheld; the prisoner mercilessly beat him. Made him gut fish in the ice room while naked, cold and hungry. When the prisoners attention was drawn the fact that Hughes couldn't take anymore punishment and that he was dying he replied, "Serves him right."

This brutal treatment continued day after day until the 22nd February, the morning was foggy. Hughes was sent on deck to make a fog signal, in doing so he accidentally spilt paraffin on the deck and a small fire started, causing £2 of damage to the boat. Wheatfill was furious he found the lad, who had gone below deck, grabbed him, dragged him back on deck saying, "You tried to kill me and I'll kill you."

The crimes behind the hangings

He then went on to kick Hughes repeatedly for 45 minutes. The kicks were so savage, that while Hughes tried to protect himself the skin on his hands was torn off. His hands damages so bad, bones were protruding. Hughes cried out, "Kill me now, I can not take no more!" Wheatfill only stopped this punishment when he was exhausted, then he ordered the lad down below to continue his duties.

Hughes was unable to walk; he was so weak from being starved and the cruel beatings, he had to crawl. The next morning he still couldn't complete his duties, he even dropped the coal for the oven, he was in a horrific state.

The other crew members had not previously come to his rescue, it seemed on that day they had woken up to the fact that Wheatfill, was slowly killing this lad with his callous and brutal treatment. They rallied round and protected Hughes throughout the course of the day, even allowing Hughes to get some rest.

The prisoner was on watch the next morning, between 4am and 5am, he ordered Hughes up on deck, and the two were alone. They were heard walking about the deck by the 3rd hand, then there was silence, then a little scuffling, then more silence. The lad Hughes was never be seen again.

Wheatfill went down to the crew and said that, "The lad has gone, I think he went overboard when trying to fetch some water." The rest of the crew dashed on deck, there was no sign of Hughes, a bucket was missing, but it was far too large a bucket for collecting water. The prisoner said to 2nd hand Peaks, "If anything transpires about this matter say you know nothing about it!"

He said the same thing to Ratzloff and offered him money to keep quiet. Ratzloff commented that the lad was a good boy, it was a pity he had gone overboard, then Wheatfill replied, "He wasn't up to much! It doesn't matter."

The case for the prosecution was that Wheatfill had purposely thrown Peter Hughes overboard on the morning of the 24th February. Witnesses were called to give evidence, it was not certain that a lifeboat was on board the vessel, but what was certain was if there was a lifeboat, it was not lowered to find the missing boy. It was law that if a member of crew went overboard, the vessel must be stopped, a lifeboat immediately launched, searches conducted, and take whatever means possible to preserve life. This clearly did not happen.

Mr. Gane summing up for the prisoner suggested that. "If having been subjected to a course of ill treatment and unlawful acts of cruelty, and if, in pursuance and continuation of such acts the boy was taken on deck by the prisoner on that fatal morning. Would it not be feasible that the boy, to avoid anymore acts of violence, had himself jumped overboard? Him rather taking his chances against the elements of the North Sea, rather than endure any more cruelty board the boat?" Adding, "If this was the case then the jury might return a verdict of manslaughter."

The judge, Mr. Justice Hawkins addressed the jury saying, "If the prisoner threw or pushed the lad overboard with a view to cause his death. Or if he had been guilty of wanton, culpable and criminal neglect of duty for the purpose of causing his death, he would be guilty of murder."

He also commented on the fact that the skipper Mr. Callan had not been called as a witness for either side and he thought it unsatisfactory that the jury did not hear his evidence.

He then went on and said. "If a man has a duty cast on him to do a particular act, if he wantonly, grossly and culpably neglects to fulfil that duty, and if by reason of that neglect, the death of another is caused, such a man would be guilty of manslaughter. But before considering any evidence you must be satisfied beyond any reasonable doubt that the boy is dead. You must not allow your minds to be prejudiced by the constant course of brutality to which the lad had been subjected to."

The jury retired to consider the verdict, an hour later they returned to the court and found the prisoner guilty of murder. The prisoner was taken to York castle jail and hanged by William Marwood on the 28th November 1882.

The crimes behind the hangings

The Times on the 13th November 1882 commented on the trial's of both Wheatfill and Brand, which is quite interesting reading. Below is the very article that was published.

On Friday there took place at York one of those trials for murder at sea, which have recently shocked society so deeply. The notorious case of 'Brand', who was hanged for the murder of a cabin boy upon a Great Grimsby smack not long ago, will be fresh in the public memory. Brand's brutality seemed at the time not likely to be paralleled; but his counterpart has been found in Edward Wheatfill, the mate of the smack Gleaner.

The Gleaner, it appears, sailed from Hull upon the 12th of January last. On board of her were the skipper and two hands, besides the prisoner, Wheatfill, and his victim, Peter Hughes, a boy of 16, who was doing the duties of cook. From the time that the vessel left Hull Wheatfill appears to have conceived, without any material reason, a spite against the unfortunate Hughes, and commended to ill treat him systematically. From a state of vigorous health, Hughes was reduced by the savagery of the mate to weakness and exhaustion.

The evidence show's that he was driven naked upon the deck, exposed to the elements of the winter in the North Sea; that he was lashed naked to the winch, and was deprived of his meals. When these and similar cruelties had rendered him incapable of doing his work, Wheatfill showed him no pity, but, on the contrary, found in his helplessness fresh occasions for brutality.

Hughes, besides being totally unnerved by ill treatment and terror, may have been naturally clumsy. A trifling act of awkwardness on his part led Wheatfill deliberately to put on his heavy sea-boots and kick Hughes about the deck until the kicker was exhausted and Hughes hands were mutilated in protecting himself. Upon the 24th of February these cruelties culminated in the tragedy of Hughes's death.

The mate and Hughes were together upon deck during the early morning watch of the former. The rest of the crew was below, and any difficulty, which there was in fixing Wheatfill with the guilt, arose from this absence of mere-witnesses. But one man heard and recognised the voices of the two together upon deck, and heard a scuffle, followed by silence. The mate came below and told the others that the boy was " gone." All rushed upon deck, but nothing was to be seen of him in the darkness.

Wheatfill's account was that the boy had fallen overboard in trying to draw some water in a bucket; but it was an important fact that the bucket, which had disappeared, Was one which Hughes would not have been likely to make use of. Wheatfill, more over, attempted to persuade or bribe the rest of the crew to hush the matter up. Hughes's disappearance could have been accounted for by several hypotheses, all more or less incriminating the prisoner. Wheatfill could have thrown or pushed the boy overboard, in which case his guilt would have been of the most complete kind. He might have terrified his victim in such a way as to lead him to jump overboard and in trust him self rather to the waves than to the merciless human being on deck. Lastly, it was possible, though improbable, that Hughes should have fallen overboard accidentally.

In this case it would have been the duty of Wheatfill to give the alarm at once and lower a boat for the purpose of rescuing him. In spite of the previous ill treatment of the boy, the question for the jury was limited to a consideration of what took place upon deck.

The jury, however, took the View that Hughes was either thrust or hunted over the vessel's side. Wheatfill was found guilty and sentenced to death. The curious point about the whole story is the conduct of the captain, Callan, during the perpetration of the atrocities, which preceded Hughes's death.

In the case of the murder of Pepper, above referred to, Brand, the murderer, was himself the captain. In every other respect the analogy between the two cases is close. The buckets of water and the heavy boots were the favourite instruments of torture both of Brand and Wheatfill. Neither Pepper nor Hughes had merited the *fire of their respective murderers. Unless maladroitness and inoffensiveness marks, out a fellow creature for hatred.*

But Brand, as the skipper of his vessel, was uncontrolled; Wheatfill was nominally subject to the orders and the restraining influence of a captain. It is intelligible that a crew should be cowed by a man like Brand, possessing the chief command, as well as, perhaps, physical strength and firearms. On the hypothesis that Wheatfill was the bully of the crew under him, their cowardice in not interposing may be overlooked; but no extenuation for the skipper's heartlessness suggests itself.

It was of course, out of the question that an indictment for manslaughter against him should be sustained. But we may at least regret, with Mr. Justice Hawkins, that he was not called either for the prosecution or the defence, so that from his evidence the jury and the public could have formed some opinion as to his conduct.

Taken together, the two cases of Brand and Wheatfill certainly suggest some unpleasant misgivings as to the conditions of life on board our coasters and fishing smacks. That two deaths should have been caused by ill treatment is a tolerably sure indication that much gross cruelty, which never comes to the public ears, is practised towards ship apprentices, cabin boys, and others in the position of Pepper and Hughes.

These dangers axe, happily, riot encountered by the greater part of our marine population. The development of our shipping has totally changed the state of things under which the cruelty commemorated by Smollett and Marryat were possible and of common occurrence.

We have wealthy owners and large companies working magnificent vessels upon systems of discipline approaching that of the Royal Navy in efficiency, and under which the risks of personal tyranny and brutality are almost eliminated.

We have Merchant Shipping Acts providing in precise and stringent terms for the welfare of sailors. The rope's and the marline-spike are now mostly obsolete on board our larger vessels. But recent experience compels the admission that the decks of smaller craft, such as coasters and fishing-smacks, are still the scenes of much fiendish cruelty.

Not that there crew is composed to any large extent of men who are capable of brutefulness. On the contrary, we believe the seafaring population of our small ports, particularly the fishing population of the East Coast, to be of simple, gentle, and pious dispositions, such as are especially endangered by their perilous calling. Their very quietness and submissiveness are probably all the more fatal when half-a-dozen of them are cooped up in a small vessel with a monster for a captain or a mate. They are cowed by his resoluteness, and so far forget their humanity as to offer no remonstrance when one of their numbers is persecuted to the verge of death. Only when the victim dies do they wake up to the fact that they have been looking on at a slow murder.

Our special shipping legislation does not provide for such contingencies. It is careful enough to secure the presence of good provisions, medicine chests, limejuice, and the like on board ships whose crews prefer a complaint. Positive cruelty and ill treatment are left to the ordinary criminal law. But the danger will always be that acts of savagery, which would never have passed unpunished upon dry land, may meet with impunity because they are enacted at sea far from the ken of justice.

The captain of the Gleaner, Callan, did stand trial for aiding and abetting the prisoner in the commission of the alleged crime, but the grand jury threw out the case and he was released unpunished.

Chapter 14 – Don't Do It Dadda!

34 year old, Joseph Laycock a Hawker from Sheffield had suffered from a disturbing past. His father and his mothers father had been found drowned, two of his uncles had committed suicide. He had a long criminal record, mostly for petty crimes such as theft and drunkenness. However he did also have a violent streak in 1879 he was arrested under suspicion of stabbing a man. He was also renowned locally as a prizefighter.

It was alleged that on two occasions he had actually tried to kill his wife. According to Maria's mother the marriage was unhappy, they would have frequent rows, this quite often resulted in violence being inflicted on Maria.

These arguments generally surfaced due to Laycock's jealousy towards his wife and were generally drink fuelled. Both Laycock and his wife were regular drinkers. Maria like Laycock would have outbursts of temper after drinking.

June 1884, Laycock was imprisoned for 21 days for a viscous assault on Maria. On being released from prison the neighbours would complain of more disturbances and arguments between the couple.

On the morning of the murders, Maria had been out collecting used prescription bottles, which could be cashed in at the pharmacy for extra money. Just after midday, due to the ensuing thunderstorm, which was hitting Sheffield at the time, she stopped collecting the medicine bottles, deciding instead to go for a drink.

Later in the afternoon she had met up with her mother who commented on her drinking and her children being left to fend for themselves. The landlord heard this discussion and asked Maria to leave. The next time she was seen, a witness said that she was fighting a woman in a local street.

Then Laycock was seen collecting his wife from another pub around 6pm that evening, this resulted in another argument in the street. A local policeman came over and told them to head off home. Although the officer did state in the witness box, that Laycock was sober at this time. This Laycock did, he went home to feed the children, but Maria headed off to her mothers to collect her brother, then go and sell the medicine bottles that she had collected.

Maria still seamed to be having a bad day, on the way back from selling the bottles; it rained again, so she and Christopher her brother stopped off at a public house to wait for the rain to slow down. When eventually it did they carried on the walk towards her mothers house, Laycock was waiting at the gate, another argument started and she ran off.

The couple was then seen together again at around 10pm, drinking at the Rawson's Arms in Tenter Street, they consumed more beer and had a bite to eat. They left the Arms and headed off back home at around 11pm; that was the last time that Maria was seen alive.

Another blazing argument started at home that night, the neighbours did nothing as this was normal behaviour with the Laycock's, and shortly after midnight a women's scream was heard, everything then went silent.

Friday 11th July, the house was in darkness, there was no sign of the Laycock's or the children, and everything was deadly silent. Three women living in the same street decided to visit the house and see if anything was wrong. They opened the door and immediately saw Maria laid face down in a pool of blood, obviously she was dead, so the women continued upstairs to investigate further.

On opening the bedroom door they saw Laycock laid on the bed, a kitchen knife at his side, blood all over, but he was still breathing. In the same bedroom were the bodies of his children, all with their throats slit, all deceased.

Sergeant Hornsey was the first policeman to arrive; he went into the kitchen before going upstairs into the bedroom. When Laycock saw him standing in the bedroom he said in a faint voice, "Let me die Bob, don't move me, just let me die." Hornsey called an ambulance and Laycock was rushed to the nearest Hospital, which was in Sheffield.

The surgeon at the local Hospital was examining Laycock when he said, "Let me die, cut my throat deeper." The surgeon went on to make a statement, saying Laycock has a serious wound to his neck, although none of the main arteries were cut, and he is in a serious condition. He arrived in a very distressed state and after being sedated he is calm.

The doctor went on to say that he has spoke about the murder, he does not know why he committed them, although he does state that he and his wife had argued, and they were both drunk. He slit her throat after she wished him dead, went upstairs and slit the oldest 3 children's throats. Taking the youngest on his knee, Joseph whom was 2 years old said, "Don't do it to me dada!"

Laycock was released from hospital on the 25th July and was immediately taken into custody and charged with the murders of Maria aged 26, Sarah Ann aged 8, Francis George aged 6, Mary Ann aged 4 and the youngest Joseph aged 2.

The trial was held at Leeds Assizes before Mr. Justice Matthew, Mr. Fenwick and Mr. C. M. Atkinson appeared for the prosecution and Mr. Meysey-Thompson conducted the defence. The prisoner while sat in the dock looked defeated and worn-out, throughout most of the trial, his head was firmly in his hands and he sobbed uncontrollably.

The result of the post-mortem was read out in court, it appeared that Maria had been covered in bruises, especially on her wrists and face, strongly suggesting that she had been beaten and restrained before the murder. One of the children had a portion of their thumb missing, this suggests that the child had been trying to protect itself.

The defence did not try to dispute any of the facts in the case, they only suggested that at the time of the murder Laycock was not responsible for his actions.

The surgeon, who had tendered his wounds in the Hospital, gave evidence that he thought the defendant could not be held accountable for his actions at that time. Neighbours and friends also gave evidence that Laycock around the time had appeared strange and not his normal self.

In the summing up to the jury, the judge said it would not be right for the jury to base its decision on the evidence of the prosecution case alone, the previous history, and the mental condition of the accused, was also an issue. He went on to state that the atrocity of the crimes committed, suggested that a sane man did not commit them.

Throughout the trial Laycock had expressed nothing but remorse, he had cried uncontrollably and begged forgiveness, for the evil deed that he had done.

The jury returned to the courtroom after only a short while and the verdict, which they all had come to an agreement on, was guilty of murder.

The judge had to pass the sentence of death by hanging. Laycock gripped the rails with both hands and spoke directly to the judge, "Thank you your worship, thank you".

The prison guards had to use a little force to prise Laycock's fingers from the rails, then they took the prisoner down the steps and away to Armley jail.

The newly appointed hangman James Billington hanged Laycock on 26th August 1884.

Chapter 15 – Dodworth Poacher

Dodworth, a village on the outskirts of Barnsley was the home James Murphy aged 45, an out of work miner and part time poacher. He had been convicted 30 or so times for poaching and had spent a 5-year sentence in prison for house breaking, previous to that; he had spent time inside prison for threatening a police sergeant. Needless to say Murphy was well known to the police, and in particular police constable Austwick who was also a resident of the village.

P.C. Austwick had served 2 or 3 summons's for poaching on Murphy over the years, and it was well known in the village that Murphy resented P.C. Austwick. Murphy had even mentioned to his circle of friends that he would do for Austwick, but these threats were laughed at, according to the policeman, Murphy was all talk and couldn't hurt anyone.

Around the end of July 1886, Murphy was in the Station Inn in the village with a few friends, he left the pub a little worse for the drink, P.C. Austwick saw him drunk in the village and reported him.

The next day Murphy was given a summons to appear in court for being drunk and riotous. Murphy was furious, later, he was in his kitchen with his friends Henry Burgess and David Sanderson, he pulled the summons from his pocket, and he waived it around and said. "Austwick will not serve another summons on any other person, I will blow a hole through him before I sleep tonight." David said to him, "Leave it, you have gotten over worse things in the past."

On Saturday 31st July, a group of men had been drinking in the Travellers Rest, after closing time; they stood around chatting before they intended to go home. A light could be seen coming towards them, it was P.C. Austwick carrying a lantern and being accompanied by another 2 men. He walked over to the men to ask them to disperse, it was late and they were getting noisy. A voice from the crowd of men said. "Oh you're here; you're the man I want." Then the man disappeared into his house, 2 minutes later he returned and said. "Where are you now?" A loud bang and a flash of light followed, the police constable fell to the floor. James Murphy put the gun into his pocket and disappeared into the night.

P.C. Austwick was laid on the pavement, a hole in his side and blood rushing through his tunic on to the floor. He was carried the 100 yards to his home by the group of men. His wife made him as comfortable as possible, the doctor was called, so were his superior officers. He died exactly two hours after being shot, he had remained conscious up until 5 minutes before he passed away.

Murphy knew the fields and woods surrounding the area better than most, the police mounted a search, but he was nowhere to be seen. Hardly surprising, he had worked the area for years as a poacher.

The police were at a loss as to where he was hiding. They searched the houses in the village, the farms and barns surrounding the village, and all the known friends, family and acquaintances of Murphy, still no sign of him.

The inquest into the shooting was heard, the cause of death was recorded as failure of the heart's action from shock and loss of blood, the result of a shot wound. Half a dozen pellets, size 5, were found lodged in the body.

Murphy was still on the run; the search area was widened, taking in the surrounding villages. The days turned into weeks, and still no sight of him. Though rumours were circulating that he had been seen in various locations close to Dodworth, but when the police investigated, there was no trace of him.

The weeks turned into months, Murphy still eluded them. They were convinced that some friend somewhere was hiding him, so they targeted whom they believed these people were, constantly turning up to search at different times of the day or night, sometimes everyday, sometimes missing a day or two.

The crimes behind the hangings

Murphy's description was passed to all the police forces in England, handbills (leaflets) were printed and distributed everywhere, a reward of one hundred Great British pounds was offered for his apprehension. Local miners joined in the search, but again he couldn't be found.

Two months after the murder, the police nearly caught Murphy. One of the houses which they visited on a regular basis, owned by Murphy's sister and her husband, Mr. & Mrs. Goss, was visited again on the 15th September, by superintendent Kane and superintendent Stansfield, along with inspector Ramsden.

While the two superintendents where talking to Maria Goss in the kitchen, Ramsden had a look around, eventually going upstairs, Murphy was in the process of jumping out of the bedroom window. Ramsden grabbed hold of him but couldn't manage to keep his grip; Murphy fell 8 feet into the garden below.

The superintendent's downstairs, ran round the back of the house, they were met by a high wall that they just couldn't get over, so Murphy made his escape. Goss and his wife were arrested and taken to Barnsley police station, where they were charged with harbouring a wanted man and remanded in custody.

The police were convinced that Murphy was hiding in disused mines in the area and the search intensified, a further 200 homes were searched. However on the Friday of the same week, information came to light that Murphy was hiding throughout the day in fields, but visited an address at Kingstone Place after dark, staying until morning.

The police took a cab to the house; sergeant's Lodge and Tideswell, searched the downstairs of the address owned by Mr. Henderson, while inspector Ramsden went upstairs. Henderson tried to push Ramsden out of the way, but Ramsden managed to get past him and went into one of the bedrooms.

To his amazement, Murphy was stood in his shirt and trousers and looked as if he had just woken up. He was trying to reach for his gun. Ramsden made a dash for him; the gun went off narrowly missing Ramsden.

Ramsden managed to get a grip on him and held onto him, until the two officers came upstairs to help. Murphy was overpowered and arrested, The Henderson's were also arrested for harbouring a felon and taken away.

Murphy appeared before the Assizes at York, Mr. Anderson prosecuted the case and Mr. Statham defended the prisoner.

Murphy pleaded guilty to murder, in his evidence he stated to the court that P.C. Austwick constantly harassed him, even going as far as questioning his children in the street. He at one time had been summonsed for doing something which he did not do, and the last summons was the final straw, he was not drunk the night Austwick said he was.

The prosecution evidence was overwhelming; they had all the men on the night of the shooting to give evidence, P.C. Austwick's own statement on the night he died, and the weapon which was recovered at the Henderson's.

The defence tried to argue that Murphy's state of mind was greatly affected by the harassment both he and his family had suffered at the hands of Auswick.

The jury however, found the prisoner guilty of murder; the judge sentenced him to death in the usual way. He was taken to York castle jail and hung by James Berry on the 9th November 1886.

Chapter 16 – The Ex Employee

55 year old Sheffield Engineer Henry Hobson had been awarded 3 good conduct badges throughout his 14 years serving in the Army. He had been employed from 1875 until late 1886 as a horn maker, for the Sheffield family owned horn makers, in Cemetery Road, Sheffield.

He had been dismissed for neglect of duty though drunkenness. Since being dismissed he had been finding it hard since then to find other suitable employment. Therefore he had turned to drink and got into vicious habits.

The family who owned the business was called the Stodhart's, Ada was the wife of John Henry Stodhart, his parents owned the company but John over saw the day to day running of the business, and was also the person who had to dismiss Henry Hobson.

Ada was at her home the morning of 23 July 1887, with her maid Florence Moseley; they were in the kitchen of the house, doing the domestic chores.

There was a knock on the door; Ada went to see whom it was. She was surprised to see Henry Hobson stood there, she knew Hobson from the factory the family owned, so she was not alarmed or frightened. Hobson politely asked if it would be possible to have a drink, as he was passing and was parched.

Ada gave him a cold glass of water, saying that she did not have anything else that she could give him. Hobson replied that water would do just fine and drank it, thanked her for her kindness then left.

Around 15 minutes later, Hobson again knocked on the door, this time he asked whether he could have a piece of rope. Ada possibly thought it was a strange request, she knew her husband had kept some in the cellar, so telling Hobson to wait she went down to find some.

Hobson seized his opportunity, for while Ada was looking downstairs, he walked into the kitchen, pulled out a pocketknife, and proceeded to attack Florence Moseley. He attempted to cut her throat, but Florence managed to protect her neck with her hand, The knife cut her badly, nearly severing her thumb. She was also bleeding from a cut to her cheek and a deep gash to her shoulder.

The commotion and the screams, coming from upstairs alerted the attention of Ada, she rushed up the steps and ran in to the kitchen. Hobson, on seeing that Ada was coming at him, stopped attacking Florence and set about apparently to do what he came for, attacking Mrs. Stodhart. Florence on being released from Hobson's grip dashed outside, down the alleyway and into the street screaming.

Ada was left in the kitchen trying to defend herself the best she could, even though Hobson was an elderly man, he was strong and quite fit. Eventually Hobson managed to get the better of Ada and slit her throat in three places.

Meanwhile Florence was running around outside in a state of complete panic, she was screaming that a man was in the house cutting everyone's throats.

A greengrocer, Mr. Hardy was passing and stopped to investigate what all the noise was about. Florence in a state of distress, panic and concern for her employer managed to inform Mr. Hardy about the man in the house. Hardy walked down the alley, just as Hobson was coming from the back of the house.

Hobson said, "He has just gone upstairs." And walked off quickly away from the house. Mr. Hardy walked in the kitchen, and straight away found Mrs. Stodhart, lying in the corner on the kitchen floor, three horrendous wounds to her throat. She managed to tell Mr. Hardy the identity of her attacker, but died shortly afterwards from her wounds.

Florence, who had managed to compose herself, came back into the house, going immediately to the room next door to thankfully, find the infant laid in the cradle unharmed.

The police came and the news of the attack quickly circulated around the village. They were searching for a man known as Henry Hobson. Some of Hobson's former work mates, also employees of Mr. Stodhart, offered to help the police in finding the man who had committed this awful crime, they placed themselves at various points along Cemetery Road, at the train station, and anywhere they thought Hobson would go.

At about 1.30pm a man called Mr. Pursglove saw Hobson near the Victoria station. Hobson appeared to have got washed and had changed his coat and vest, he looked like he was just going for a stroll, not like someone that had committed a murder and was fleeing.

Mr. Pursglove pointed out Hobson to police constable Ford. Ford ran over to Hobson, grabbed him and placed him under arrest, then transported him to the central police station. When Hobson was charged with the murder his only reply was, "That's a caution?"

Florence was taken to the hospital for immediate medical attention, as she was the only eyewitness to the attack, her evidence was vital for the prosecution. She recovered enough to attend court for the trial of Hobson, although she was still injured she gave evidence as to the events of the 23rd July.

The jury found the prisoner guilty of murder. His lordship sentenced him to death by hanging, which was performed by James Billington on the 22nd August 1887 at Armley jail.

Chapter 17 – Broken Brush

William Berridge was the foreman of the Brick and Carbon makers, at Dodsworth Road, Barnsley, South Yorkshire, working for the company for 11 years. On the morning of the 21st March 1888, James Richardson aged 23 had worked at the factory for 5 years clocked on for work at the usual time and went to the carbon room where he was employed as a Labourer.

Mr. Berridge came into the room and saw Richardson sweeping up with a sweeping brush, which had accidentally been broken a few days previously. He asked Richardson why the brush was broken, Richardson explained that it had been an accident, but Mr. Berridge for some reason did not believe his account. He accused Richardson of breaking it on purpose and dismissed him, telling him to come back later for his wages. Richardson threw down the brush grabbed his coat, yelled back at Mr. Berridge and left the building, going straight home. After having breakfast he put on his coat and left the house to go and collect his wages from the works.

Richardson arrived back at the factory, finding that Mr. Berridge was in the general office with the owner of the business Mr. Chamberlain. They were in the inner office, in the process of a meeting. James Richardson came into the office and asked if he could speak to Mr. Berridge.

Berridge left the inner office closely followed by Mr. Chamberlain, who noticed that when the foreman walked by Richardson, he looked greatly agitated.

Both men walked outside in to the yard, Mr. Chamberlain still following the men. A few seconds later Mr. Chamberlain heard a gun shot, he looked over and saw Richardson pointing a pistol at Berridge. The visibility was bad due to smoke from the chimney, but it looked to Mr. Chamberlain that Richardson had fired at Mr. Berridge's legs.

A couple of seconds later, two more shots were heard, Mr. Berridge fell to the ground, Richardson tried to run down the road.

Mr. Chamberlain managed to catch him and asked him what he had done. Richardson reply was. "I must have been mad, I will deliver myself up." Mr. Chamberlain grabbed Richardson then escorted him to the nearest police station.

Mr. Berridge was rushed to hospital and died from his injuries just over a week later. James Richardson was charged with the murder on 1st April, he appeared at the Leeds Assizes for trial on 3rd May 1888. Mr. Banks and Mr. C. M. Atkinson prosecuted the case; Mr. C. Mellor led the defence.

Dr. Blackburn, who had conducted the post mortem said in his evidence that he found two pistol bullets in the body of Mr. Berridge, one in the lower part of the body and the other in the skull, this was the one which caused death. The remarkable thing was how Mr. Berridge had managed to survive for as long as he did.

Richardson made a touching and emotional statement to the jury, in it he said. "I was dismissed for something that I did not do, this preyed on my mind. I went home, while walking there I put my hand in my pocket, to find wrapped in a handkerchief the pistol that I had purchased on 5th November last. The bullets where in the gun for save keeping. I decided that after I had got my wages I would go and sell the pistol."

He went on to say. "Berridge had been out to get me for months, while walking in the yard he put his finger in my cheek and shoved against me, I felt a terrible sensation in my head. I do not recollect anything more until Mr. Chamberlain spoke to me."

Richardson, when he finished his statement, took his seat in the dock and completely broke down.

Mr. Mellor on behalf of Richardson, insisted that Richardson had received great provocation, the offence had been committed under duress, and under circumstances that should reduce the charge to manslaughter.

The jury retired to consider the verdict, after deliberating for only 20 minutes they returned back to the courtroom and found the prisoner guilty of murder, with a strong recommendation of mercy.

The judge sentenced James Richardson to the death sentence and James Billington executed him at Armley jail 17 days later on the 25th May 1888.

Chapter 18 – Huddersfield Groom

Charles and Elizabeth Bulmer lived in Huddersfield, they had been married for 12 years; the marriage seemed to be doomed from the start. Bulmer, who was a groom, worked hard through the day, but at evenings and weekends he would go out drinking.

This nearly always led to arguments and the ill treatment of his wife. When sober he was a nice fellow and treated his wife very nicely. Elizabeth was a respectable hardworking woman, worked as a mill hand at the local mill, and seemed to be well liked by her work colleagues and neighbours.

The couple separated many times over the years, due to Bulmer's drinking. Elizabeth twice made complaints against him to the police for his brutality against her on both occasions, November 1887 and May 1888, he was bound over to keep the peace or he would be imprisoned.

On the September 5th 1888, Bulmer had been drinking as normal, he returned home, an argument started and he threatened to kill his wife. Elizabeth wasn't going to put up with his behaviour anymore, so she threw him out and told him not to return again, she had had enough.

Bulmer went to stay at a friend's of his near Lockwood, Huddersfield, not too far away from the family home. Bulmer remained quiet for a while, he left his wife alone and stayed away from the public houses.

On the 10th September, he had a conversation with a friend, the topic being hanging and whether they suffered at the gallows etc. Then he went for a drink and a walk to clear his head. After leaving the pub while on his walk, he passed Elizabeth in the street.

She was talking to a Mrs. Bailey and the young man who was due to marry Elizabeth's daughter from her previous marriage. Bulmer asked her if he could come round and get his clothes. Elizabeth said he could as long as he brought a police constable with him, so there was not going to be any trouble. Bulmer agreed and off he went to find a policeman.

Police constable Callaghan was approached by Bulmer not long afterwards, he was asked if he would accompany him to Elizabeth's house, which he agreed to do. When they arrived there Elizabeth wasn't back and they couldn't gain access.

P.C. Callaghan told Bulmer to go home and he would go back with him again the next day, when he was on duty again. He agreed to do so walked off down the street.

He went into the public house and had a couple of drinks. While drinking, the rumours of his wife having a relationship with another man got round to Bulmer, he couldn't believe what he was hearing. He finished his beer then set off back to see Elizabeth. He arrived at her house around 9.30pm Elizabeth reluctantly allowed him in, an argument started and around 9.45pm a scream which woke up to neighbour's children was heard.

Mrs. Bailey the neighbour went round to the house to find Elizabeth dead on the floor, blood spewing out of 4 gaping holes in her throat, her head was nearly chopped off through the severity of the wounds. Charles Bulmer was nowhere to be seen.

Bulmer had left the house, visited a friend's house to clean himself off from the blood, and even gone as far as giving two razors to his friend's eldest son, one that was covered in blood. Then he took himself back down to the public house. It was here that he met a man called Mr. Lewis. Bulmer told him what had happened at the home of Elizabeth and asked him if he would go and see if she was dead.

Meanwhile back at the house, the police had been called and Elizabeth was certified dead. Mr. Lewis arrived saying that Bulmer was drinking at the pub down the road. The police went to arrest him, but he was nowhere to be seen.

Much later that evening, after the pubs had shut, Charles Bulmer walked in to the police station in Huddersfield and gave himself up. He was charged with the murder of Elizabeth Bulmer, remanded in prison after the preliminary hearing and appeared at the NorthEastern Assizes in Leeds on the 13th November 1888.

The trial in front of Mr. Justice Sir Baron Charles Pollock had Mr. Harold and Mr. Binks prosecuting and Mr. Fox defending the prisoner.

The defence stated that Bulmer on that evening had no plans to murder his wife, the murder was totally without premeditation. Bulmer did not murder his wife through a fit of jealousy nor were the allegations that his wife was keeping male company true, therefore the crime should be reduced to manslaughter.

The jury however found Bulmer guilty of murder and the death sentence was passed.

At the prison Bulmer called for the governor, Capt. Keane and strongly denied to him that his wife was intimate with another man. Though he did admit the justice of the sentence that he was due to meet.

James Billington executed Bulmer aged 51 on New Years day 1889 at Armley jail.

Chapter 19 – The Showman

Travelling showman Robert West his wife and children worked the feats and fairs around the north of England. West ran the shooting gallery stall; he had been married to Emma for 13 years in a happy and harmonious relationship.

Then in August 1888 he met a man nicknamed 'Leicester Jack' and over the weeks that ensued Robert started to change, he became moody, argumentative, depressed and violent. Emma had had enough and the couple separated. Emma packed her belongings and took the children and moved in with her mother who lived in Derbyshire.

Robert kept in touch with this wife and children over the fore coming months, he was trying to change, he kept asking his wife to forgive him and to start again with a clean slate. Eventually Emma agreed and she moved back into his caravan with him.

To all the other showmen, they seemed a happy couple working and living together, enjoying each other's company, all thoughts of their previous differences had seem to have been forgotten.

Early August 1888, the family were working the feast at Clay Cross and then it set off to Sheffield to work the Hansworth - Woodhouse Fair, a few miles outside of the centre of Sheffield.

They arrived at Woodhouse on the 12th August 1888, Robert telling his wife and eldest child to take the caravan to the campsite; he was going into Sheffield to buy some prizes for the shooting gallery.

Returning from Sheffield in a cab, he dropped off his purchase's, he then went to the Royal Hotel and then onto the Cross Daggers public house for a drink. At 10pm that evening he was seen drinking with another showman called Mr. Law, he appeared drunk and apparently in great distress of the mind.

His wife later joined him that evening at the public house, and then they were later seen at the campsite both under the influence of drink, but quite friendly and not argumentative.

Everything seemed quiet throughout that night, no quarrels or any form of disturbance were heard from fellow showman, even though the caravans were sited close to each other.

Around 5.30am Robert West went to a neighbouring caravan, owned by a man called Warwick, and informed him that a quarrel had taken place and he had killed his wife.

Warwick and another man rushed round to the West's caravan, and found Emma West laid on the bed, her throat had been cut, the wound being around 5" long and very deep. Her baby was asleep and laid next to the bed in the cot undisturbed. The knife, covered in blood was laid on the floor. The bed, walls and floor were also covered in blood.

The police were called and sergeant Ford arrived at the scene, West immediately handed himself over to Sgt. Ford and made a full confession. Saying that he and Emma had a quarrel, she had said words that had enraged him so much he picked up the knife, and cut her throat. Adding that he was tired of living and wished he could finish himself off. According to Sgt. Ford, West was callous and indifferent throughout making his statement.

The body of Mrs. West was taken to the George Inn Hotel to await the police surgeon, and the caravan was also taken to the Yard of the same Inn for a complete search to be performed. The police surgeon stated that the fatal wound had severed the carotid artery and the jugular vein. A sharp knife had caused this, like the one found at the scene.

Robert West was charged with the murder of Emma West and appeared at the Assizes. Mr. Kershaw and Mr. Palmer represented him. The prosecution on behalf of the crown was Mr. Banks and Mr. Whitaker Thompson.

Robert West's sister gave evidence in court to the effect that the family had for generations succumbed to mental problems, and her parents were cousins.

The defence said that evidence showed that the crime was done in a moment of insanity, therefore the prisoner should not be found guilty of murder.

The jury found the prisoner guilty of murder, but recommended mercy.

The learned judge passed sentence of death in the usual way. James Billington executed West aged 45 in a double execution along side Frederick Brett on the 31st December 1889 at Armley jail.

The crimes behind the hangings

Chapter 20 – Halifax Railwayman

Finding employment in the 19th century was not easy, you had to go where to work was, this often involved moving away from home, leaving you family behind, or taking your family with you.

Frederick Brett aged 39 managed to secure employment at the Halifax Railway Company in 1889. He packed up his belongings and along with his wife Margaret, they moved to a lodging house near his new work place, which was owned by James Hindley.

The first couple of weeks living at the lodging house seemed happy, the couple kept themselves busy exploring the new area when Brett wasn't working. He would take Margaret down to the local public house on a Saturday night, both returning quite early and retiring to their room until the following morning.

Then things started to take a turn for the worse. The couple started drinking heavily which always seemed to result in arguments. Brett started being jealous of his wife, she was meeting new friends throughout the day while he was at work, and he didn't like it.

Then the arguments started getting violent, serious threats were made towards his wife. The landlord Mr. Hindley on two occasions told the Brett's to leave. He ran a quiet happy lodging house, and they were disturbing the other guests. Margaret always apologised for her husband's behaviour, and persuaded the landlord to allow the couple to stay, on the condition that their behaviour changed.

On the night of the 19th October, the couple had been out drinking, and returned back home around 11.30pm. Brett had consumed quite a lot to drink and was in an argumentative mood.

Mr. Hindley heard him say to his wife, "You treat me lightly, if you don't want me, let me go at once." Margaret told him to shut up and go to bed.

The next morning, Margaret got up as normal, made Brett his breakfast, took it upstairs for him. Then she aired and ironed his clothes for the day. The couple seemed to be on good terms throughout that morning.

Dinner was made and eaten in the dining room at 12.30pm. The couple sat happily chatting and helped to clear way the used plates. Then Brett sent out for some beer, he drank 2 quarts of beer between 12.30 and 2.30pm, he appeared to be quite drunk.

Around 5pm he ordered his wife to accompany him upstairs for an afternoon snooze. Margaret reluctantly went, and all was quite for a couple of minutes.

Almost immediately Mr. Hindley heard Margaret scream out, "Jim, Jim." He ran upstairs, and went straight into the couple's bedroom. He wasn't prepared for what he saw, Brett was laid on the top of his wife, and blood was gushing out of a gaping hole in her throat. Brett was holding a pruning knife in his hand. Both the knife and his hands were covered in blood. Mr. Hindley ran back downstairs to raise the alarm, the front door was locked and the key missing.

Mr. Hindley, went back to the bedroom to get the key from Brett, he must have taken it as all the other lodgers had gone out for the afternoon. Brett gave him the key and said, "It's done now and can't be undone. She was a good lass to me."

The police were called and Brett was arrested. Margaret had died almost instantly, nothing could have been done to save her life, and Brett was charged with the murder of his wife.

At the Assizes in Leeds, Mr. Harold Thomas prosecuted the case and Mr. Charles Mellor defended the prisoner. Mr. Justice Manisty was the presiding judge.

The case was an easy case to prosecute, Mr. Hindley, gave his evidence that the couple had gone upstairs to bed, a minute or two later Margaret screamed, and he caught Brett with the knife in his hand.

The defence did not contest any of the evidence, they did however suggest that Brett had been provoked by his wife's recent behaviour and asked the jury to find the prisoner guilty of manslaughter.

The jury without hesitation found the prisoner guilty of murder and Mr. Justice Manisty passed the death sentence in the normal way.

James Billington carried out the execution on the 31st December 1889. Brett was accompanied to the gallows by a Roman Catholic Priest, he made no comment before the trap was released, he died alongside Robert West also a wife murderer, in the first double execution performed inside the prison walls, and only the second such execution at Armley jail.

Chapter 21 – Bowling Murder

Mrs. Duckworth, who lived at Lord Street, Bowling, near Bradford, had adopted James Harrison. She had brought Harrison up as her own child. He vowed to look after her in her twilight years. Even though he had been married to Hannah for the past 13 years and they had children, they all lived with Mrs. Duckworth, so he could look after her like she had done him.

Harrison was described as an easy going and hard working man; he worked in the dye room at the local mill in Bradford. He was kind and generous, always giving his mother and wife money on payday. He loved spending time with his children, being a very affectionate and kind father.

Hannah on the other hand, even though she was hard working, she worked in a local mill, she had a quick vile temper and would always provoke her husband, even going as far as to be-little him in company.

On the morning of 12th May, Harrison got out of bed and went downstairs to light the coal fire. He and his wife the previous night had quarrelled. Hannah had said some nasty things to him.

This must have been preying on his mind while lighting the fire, he grabbed a poker, went upstairs and grabbed his wife by the neck; a struggle ensued eventually leading to Harrison hitting her over the head 2 or else 3 times. Hannah fell to the ground and died shortly afterwards.

The police were called and Harrison made a full confession and was charged with the murder of his wife. His trial was heard at the West Yorkshire Assizes in Leeds on the 6th August 1890.

The judge being Mr. Justice Charles. Mr. Harold Thomas and Mr. Longstaffe, were the prosecutors, and Mr. Mellor conducted the defence.

The crimes behind the hangings

The doctor, who had performed the post-mortem on Hannah, disclosed in evidence to the court that Hannah's skull had been fractured in three places.

James Harrison pleaded guilty of murder, and the defence tried to show how, over the years he had been married, the diabolical way his wife had treated him.

The jury found the prisoner guilty of murder, with the recommendation to the judge for mercy due to extreme provocation. The learned judge was having none of it and sentenced the defendant to death by hanging.

He was taken away to Armley jail to await his final journey to the gallows. An appeal was lodged, but this failed, and a petition was sent to the Home Office for a reprieve, this also fell on deaf ears.

The 26th August 1890, James Harrison who was 32 years old, ate a hearty breakfast and smoked his pipe; James Billington came into the condemned cell, pinioned his arms and legs before leading him to the gallows and carried out the execution.

Chapter 22 – Police Killer

Market gardener, husband and father Robert Kitching aged 34, lived in the village of Leeming, near Bedale, North Yorkshire. Police sergeant James Weedy, was a member of the North Riding of Yorkshire police force, was stationed at, and also lived at Leeming.

On the evening of 19th September 1890, Robert Kitching decided that he was going to go out for a couple of beers down at the Leeming Bar public house. He pulled up outside the public house and left his pony and trap outside.

Later the same evening Sgt. Weedy came to the pub and seeing that the pony and trap was unattended, he went inside. Spotting Kitching drinking with some other men, Sgt. Weedy asked Kitching if he could have a word with him outside. Kitching reluctantly agreed and both men stepped outside.

Sgt. Weedy advised Kitching that it was illegal to leave a horse and cart unattended, and due to the amount of alcohol that he had consumed, he advised him that he would be better off going home. Kitching would have done of it, he fully intended on going back into the pub, and if Weedy didn't leave him be, he would shoot him.

When the public house closed Kitching headed of home, he was quite drunk and had, since the conversation with the police sergeant been argumentative with other customers in the public house.

When he arrived home, an argument started between him and his wife, Kitching went to find his gun, so his wife grabbed her young children, who were dressed only in their nightclothes, and fled to a neighbour.

Around 11pm that same evening, Kitching turned up at his father in law's house in Leeming, the house was in darkness. Kitching kept on banging on the door until Mr. Caygill woke up and came down to see what all the commotion was about. Kitching, well and truly drunk seemed to be scared and excited, he went into the kitchen and said, "I have shot Sgt. Weedy." Mr. Caygill and his son couldn't believe what they were hearing, the best course of action they thought, was to take Kitching back home and let him sleep it off.

Arriving at the Kitchings house, Mr. Caygill went into the kitchen. On the table were tins containing gunpowder and shot, some empty cartridges were also laid around.

Kitching pointed to the gate to his land, saying, "He is over yonder, I need to put it on the road so people think someone trailed him and attacked him."

At this time Caygill's son and Kitching left the house and went and carried the body on to the road and hid it out of sight. Kitching then went to his shed and got the gun out that he had shot Sgt. Weedy with, he walked down the field and threw the gun in to the stream hoping that no one would find it.

The next morning Sgt. Weedy was found, his body was examined and found to have a gunshot wound to the neck, which had been fired from close range. The wound according to experts had caused immediate death.

There was no gunpowder upon the deceased nor were there any indications that a struggle had taken place, either on the deceased or on the nearby land. The body had obviously been shot elsewhere and after death moved to the location where it was found.

A witness called Mr. Wood came and told the police that he had seen Sgt. Weedy around 10.40pm the previous evening, he was heading towards Kitching's home to interview him about his drunken conduct at the pub that evening.

Sgt. Weedy's body had been found just yards from the gate that led to the Kitching's home. Along with the statement made by Mr. Wood, Kitching was the obvious suspect. They rushed up the driveway leading to Kitching's house, to arrest him and bring him for questioning, but hardly surprisingly, Kitching was not at home nor did he return that day.

The police searched for him in all his usual haunts throughout that day; eventually they received information that Kitching would be at the Richmond Market the next day. They went to the market and waited for him to arrive. Kitching walked round the corner, the police jumped out of their hiding places and he was subsequently arrested.

On charging him with the murder, Kitching's only comment was. "What me! You cannot blame me!"

The Assizes at York in December 1890 before Mr. Justice Lawrence was the setting for the trial. Mr. Luck and Mr. Meed prosecuted the case, while Mr. Waddy represented the defendant.

Mr. Waddy said that; Sgt. Weedy appeared at the gate to Kitching's home and grabbed the prisoner, a struggle then took place, with resulted in the gun going off accidentally, which tragically resulted in the death of the police officer.

The jury however did not believe this story and found Kitching guilty of murder but they did recommend mercy. His lordship, as court protocol instructs, asked Kitching, "If there was anything that he wanted to say before the death sentence was passed?"

Kitching said, "Weedy was shot accidentally, I was holding the gun pointed in the air, Weedy rushed at me and struck me with a stick. A struggle then took place, during which the gun went off accidentally."

The judge passed sentence of death on the prisoner and added, "Although the recommendation for mercy will be passed onto the proper quarter, I do not hold out any hope of mercy being granted."

No reprieve had been given when James Billington arrived at York castle on the 29th December 1890, and hanged Kitching the following day.

The crimes behind the hangings

Chapter 23 – Gruesome Murder

The courthouse at Leeds was packed to full capacity on the 30th July 1891. Two defendants were in the dock; their names were Walter Lewis Turner aged 32 and his mother Ann Turner aged 58.

Mr. Harold Thomas and Mr. Edmondson were conducting the prosecution. Mr. C. Mellor and Mr. Palmer represented the two prisoners. The clerk of the court read out the charges to the court, which were; On the 6th June 1891 they murdered Barbara Whitham Waterhouse at Horsforth near Leeds. They were also charged with the lesser crime of being accessories after the fact.

Before the prisoners were given the opportunity to give their pleas to the charges, the learned judge suggested that it would be a good idea to hear the lesser charge first. Mr. Thomas agreed to this course of action be adapted. Mr. Mellor then applied to the court that the prisoner's be tried separately, after a great deal of discussion, this was also agreed.

Walter Turner was removed from the dock, and taken away to the jail to await his trial. His mother on the other hand, remained in the dock and the charge of being an accessory after the fact to the murder of the child, by some person or person's unknown was read out to her.

Mr. Thomas then addressed the jury to the facts of the case.

"Barbara was a six-year-old girl who lived with her parents in Horsforth. On June 6th last, Barbara was last seen at 1.30pm, after a widespread search she wasn't found. The prisoner and her son lived in Horsforth not far from the home of Mr. and Mrs. Waterhouse. On the night of the 10th June the dead, mutilated body was found near the Town hall buildings, not far from where we stand today. The body was wrapped in a shawl, which belonged to the prisoner. There were 46 stab or cut wounds to the body of Barbara, one which was 15 to 18 inches in length and extending from the neck downwards in the front of the body."

The statement that Mrs. Turner had made to the police was read out to the court:
"I have a son named Walter turner he is 32 years old a weaver by trade, I returned home from visiting family on the 6th June, there was a sofa in front of the coal place under the stairs. Walter spent all day on the sofa, never moving from it when someone else was around. It seemed strange but I didn't suspect anything. I suffer from dreams that normally come true, I awoke early the next morning, thinking that something was wrong in the house, I moved the sofa and looked in the coal shed. I saw a bundle of clothes, when I touched them they were cold and a smell was coming from them. Walter came up behind me and said that he didn't do it, he was just hiding it for a friend. I bought some lime powder to disguise the smell. I went round to Mrs. Cotterill's house and told her that what I had seen. Walter borrowed a tin box and we moved the bundle to Leeds and then on the night of the 10th June, we emptied the box behind the town hall where it was found. Then we took the box to Leeds station where we left it."

Inspector Sowerby, who had taken the statement from Turner said, "As soon as the statement was signed we took the prisoner to the spot where she described leaving the body, she immediately pointed and said that's where Walter turned it out of the box. We then went to the Train station and the box was where she said she it would be."

Mrs. Cotterill said that. "Mrs. Turner came round and said that there's nothing less than murder at our house, she described to us what she had seen, both me and my husband advised her to go to the police or we would."

Mr. Mellor addressed the jury on Turners behalf, he urged that her conduct showed that she was not attempting to protect anyone from the consequences of this offence. She told relatives and friends all that she knew.

The learned judge said, "The question for the jury was, whether the prisoner had endeavoured to screen the murderer of the child, by an attempt to get rid of the body. The evidence given by the prosecution was not doubtful."

The jury returned the verdict of guilty, with a strong recommendation of mercy; the judge said, notwithstanding the recommendation of the jury, he felt it was his duty to inflict the heaviest punishment allowed by law. He then passed the sentence of penal servitude for life with hard labour.

August 2nd 1891, the case was due to open with Walter Turner in the dock for being an accessory after the murder. The jury had been sworn in when the prosecution offered no evidence against the prisoner and the case was dismissed. They did however plan on pursuing the case of murder against the prisoner. This charge was allowed to go ahead by the judge, and the case commenced.

At the close of Mr. Thomas's opening speech, outlining the case to the jury, he stated that he would be calling to give evidence the prisoner's mother Ann Turner. Mr. Mellor immediately objected to this witness saying, "Ann Turner is charged along with her son with the murder, the evidence she gives would either prejudice the case against her or against her son."

The judge asked the jury to remove themselves from the court, while the barristers discussed this matter of law. Mr. Thomas addressed the judge that, in the case of Ann Turner, they were satisfied with the conviction of being an accessory after the murder, they would not be offering any evidence in the matter of murder against her. The judge thought it would be wise to discuss this matter in private in his chambers, the case was adjourned for a short while.

A short while later, a new jury was sworn into court, the defendant in the dock was Ann Turner answering the charge of murder, the charge was read out, the prosecution stood and offered no evidence to support the charge. The judge therefore dismissed the case and released the jury. Ann Turner however was not released, she was taken down to the cells, to wait to be called to give evidence against her son, then she would be transported to prison for the rest of her life.

The trial then continued with Walter Turner in the dock, Inspector Sowerby and Mrs. Cotterill were called and their evidence was the same as in the trial of Mrs. Turner.

Medical evidence was heard, the same evidence that was given in the Inquest into the murder on the 12th June by Mr. Ward. He, with the aid of a diagram, described the 45 wounds which had been inflicted, some of them were superficial, whilst others were off a shocking nature. His opinion was the wound to the chest had caused death.

The wounds to the other side of the body were then described; he was of the opinion that an attempt had been made to carve the letter A onto the body. A wound on the girl's middle finger had bled; this clearly shows that it was inflicted while she was alive and likely to be the result of her defending herself.

The wound to the chest and finger were the only wounds that bled therefore they were the only wounds that were made while the little girl was alive. There were no cuts on the girls clothing corresponding to the wounds to the body, therefore, the clothes had been removed or pulled over the girls head, before the body was mutilated. It was in his opinion that the girl had bled to death.

There was no proof that there had been any other interference to the body, but the appearance of the body strongly suggested that, this was the motive.

The weapon used would have been a blade of around two and half inches in length. Many of the 40 or so wounds, would, if they had been inflicted during life, have been sufficient to cause death.

At the inquest he had said that death possibly would have taken place around 60 hours before the body was found, he now believes that it might have been even longer.

The medical evidence was supported by Dr. Jacob one of the Honorary Physicians at Leeds infirmary and also Mr. Archbold, Honorary demonstrator of anatomy at the Yorkshire College.

Police sergeant Herbert Toyser stationed at Horsforth police station gave evidence regards to the arrest of the prisoner. "We got word from Leeds police station that Mrs. Turner had given a statement indicting her son, for both the murder and the disposal of the body of little Barbara. I visited the house, knocked on the door. I got no reply, so eventually I broke in and found Turner alone in the house. He looked white and was shaking; he was holding a newspaper, which had an article about the finding of the body. I said to him that I was arresting him in connection with the murder of Barbara Whitehouse, he replied, 'What grounds have you for charging me with it?' I said so much that I shall apprehend you, and take you to the superintendent's office. He then said, 'You'll have to prove it.' I placed him in irons and took him away."

The case came to a close for the prosecution; they summed up the evidence to the jury. "The prisoner took the girl from where she was playing in Horsforth, he killed her and hid her body at the house he shared with his mother. When she discovered his hiding place, they both put the body in a metal container, carried to container to a cousins house in Leeds where it was left a couple of days. They then put the body behind the town hall and left the box at the train station. The evidence clearly shows that Mrs Turner knew what was in the box, therefore the prisoner knew. He knew because he had killed the girl."

Mr. Mellor then addressed the jury on behalf of the prisoner; he pointed out that the prisoner had never once been seen with the murdered child. None of his clothes contained any traces of blood, he added, although the prisoner maybe as guilty as his mother of disposing the body, there was no evidence that could justify the jury into returning a verdict of murder. It could have been quite easy for any tramp, after murdering the child, to have placed the body in the coal shed of the accused house. The general opinion of the residents of Horsforth was a stranger had committed the murder.

He went on to show evidence that a tramp called Mark Ibbotson was arrested near Stockport, Lancashire, at 5am on the morning of the 12th June. He had given his address as 6 Harper's Court,

Graper Street, Leeds. He made a statement under oath, that he had committed the murder of Barbara Whitehouse. However a local surgeon pronounced him as insane, and he is now in the Parkside Asylum, near Macclesfield.

On the Wednesday after Barbara went missing a letter was sent to the girls father, it was sent by a lady in Huddersfield and said, 'Since the child has gone missing I have been to Horsforth, and met a woman who was a tramp. She had with her a little girl, whom was obviously not the daughter of the tramp. She begged a penny and the little girl was made to say thank you.'

A Leeds milkman and his wife were walking home on the Wednesday evening at about 10.30, they met a gentlemanly-looking man, wearing a tall hat, and he seemed to be carrying a bundle quite gingerly. This brought the remark from the milkman that maybe it was a body. The next morning he had while on his rounds heard that Barbara had been found near the town hall, so he went straight to the police station and made a statement.

Mr. Malcolm the coroner had even said himself, at the inquest that. "From the appearance of the body it was evident that a very foul murder had been committed. Personally, he did not abandon the idea that it would ultimately be found that the crime itself was not committed in the borough."

The judge in his summing up said the murder of the child, by whomsoever it was committed, was one of terrible atrocity. He took upon himself the entire responsibility of the course that he had adopted in, by firstly placing the prisoner's mother on her trial for being an accessory after the fact.

He added that it was a strange thing that the prisoner could not give any account whatsoever as to how the dead body of the child had been placed in the cellar. The child was alive on the Saturday; the sofa was placed over the door on the Sunday, so as to prevent anyone from discovering the contents of the cellar. The greater portion of that day the prisoner had his meals on the sofa.

On Monday the dead body was found and on the Wednesday, the prisoner and his mother moved the body. He also called to the jury's attention the reaction of the prisoner when the police came to his house.

The jury retired to consider there verdict at 6pm that afternoon, they returned back in to court 15 minutes later and announced that they found the prisoner guilty of murder. The judge asked Turner if he had anything to say before sentence was passed, he said. "I wish to assert my innocence, as I have always done and as I always shall."

The judge after putting on the black cap said, "You have been properly convicted of the most atrocious crime it had ever been my lot to try. If the people amongst whom he had lived had got hold of him, he would probably have met his death at their hands. Had they seen the photograph of the dead body of the murdered child, no power on earth would have prevented them from tearing him limb from limb."

He then passed the sentence of death in the usual way. Cheers and applause were to be heard in the courtroom, but was quickly stopped by the judge as the prisoner was led away.

James Billington executed Turner on the 18th August 1891. Turner did not make any further statements, taking with him, what really happened to Barbara and why, to his grave.

The newspapers had covered the story of Barbara Whitehouse and her disappearance, through to the finding of the body and the subsequent trials of the accused.

The public was shocked and appalled at the crime that Walter Turner had committed, but they were also shocked with the sentence that Ann Turner had been given. What mother wouldn't do anything she could to help her son in trouble?

Petitions were signed and presented to the Home Secretary, Mrs. Turner's sentence was later reduced to 12 months imprisonment with hard labour.

Chapter 24 – The Barmaid

The landlady of the Ivy Bridge public house left the pub 2pm on the afternoon of the 21st August 1892, to nip into Huddersfield to do some shopping. She left the bar in the capable hands of her waitress; a girl called Catherine Dennis. Kate has she liked to be called was an Irish girl, 16 years of age had worked for Mrs. Brook, the landlady for nearly a year.

The only customer in the public house at that particular time was 26 year old James Stockwell. He was sat in the kitchen eating a pie using a sharp knife.

John Iredale came for a drink at 3pm, nobody else was in the bar area apart from the waitress Kate, and he stayed for around 15 minutes before leaving and heading home. As he left two men passed him and walked into the public house.

The local butchers boy attempted to gain entry at 4pm that afternoon, the place was locked up being alarmed at this, he called over to a neighbour, and they both managed to force entry into the establishment. They made a shocking discovery; Kate was laid on the floor dead, stabbed in the neck.

The police were immediately called and went to the scene to investigate, upon hearing about the murder Mr. Iredale, rushed round to the police station and gave a statement regarding to the two men he had seen earlier.

Mrs. Brook's came back from shopping, her pub full of police and a dead waitress, was a sight that she hadn't been prepared for, she was hysterical.

The police did manage to get the name of James Stockwell, who had been in the kitchen earlier, from her. They sent officers to try and trace the two strangers that Mr. Iredale had informed them about, and also went round to Stockwell's home to question him.

The two men were soon picked up for questioning, even though one of the men was carrying a knife, they managed to satisfy the police that they were innocent and they were released. The hunt was on for Stockwell who was now the main suspect, he had vanished from his home, nobody had seen him. Unperturbed the police kept looking and searching, knowing that he would eventually turn up.

Days later, the 7th September, Mrs. Stockwell, the mother of James was awoken early in the morning by a noise on her stairway; she jumped out of bed to find James standing on the landing.

She asked if he had anything to do with the murder, he replied that he did not. She went on to say that, whatever the circumstances or the consequences he must tell the police the truth, they have been looking for him for days he must turn himself in. James said that he would tell the truth, so Mrs. Stockwell went and fetched police constable Taylor from nearby.

Taylor came to arrest Stockwell, he offered no resistance, and was taken to the police station for questioning. In interview he was asked where he had been for the last 12 days, Stockwell replied that he had been hiding on the moors, he had been sleeping under haystacks on different farms. Not having eaten for several days he was tired of running, exhausted and hungry, he just wanted to give himself up.

He confessed to the murder and was taken to the Magistrates court the same day to be committed for trial at the Assizes. The charge was read out in court, and Stockwell was asked how he pleaded. "Guilty." He mumbled, the magistrate could not hear, so he was asked again. This time he replied in a much louder tone of voice.

He was remanded into the custody of the county police. A few days later he was brought before the County Bench and they remanded him again into custody, he was taken to Wakefield jail to await his trial.

There were large crowds on the route from the court, feelings were running high, many people shouting, "lynch him, lynch him." Eventually the police managed to get Stockwell to Wakefield and out of harms way.

The case was heard at the Leeds Assizes before Mr. Justice Charles. Mr. Harold Thomas and Mr. Edmondson prosecuted on behalf of the treasury the prisoner was represented by Mr. C. Mellor and Mr. C.F. Palmer.

The facts of the case according to the prosecution were that, the prisoner had spent the day drinking in the Ivy Bridge public house. During the day he had some refreshment and used his pocket-knife, around 4pm that afternoon he had left the public house, the body was then found shortly afterwards, her throat had been cut with a knife.

The prisoner fled Linthwaite, going into hiding on the moors. When he was captured at his mother's house and taken to the police station he made a statement of his own free will to the police, this statement says.

"The girl had been tormenting me and pulling my hair, and in a moment of passion I ran after her and got hold of her, there is not point going round about it, I may as well get it over with, it was all through drink".

The jury took ten minutes to deliberate and found the prisoner guilty of murder; he was sentenced to death.

Billington arrived at Armley prison on the afternoon of the 4th January 1992, stayed the night to prepare, and hanged James Stockwell the next morning.

Chapter 25 – Holbeck Murder

The courtroom on the 26th May 1892 was packed to full capacity. The learned judge, Mr. Justice Charles was seated. The prosecution consisting of Mr. Harold Thomas and Mr. Whitaker Thompson were sat waiting for the prisoner Henry Pickering aged 29 to be brought up from the cells into the dock. The seat reserved for the defending council was unoccupied.

Pickering arrived from the court cells, which were located in police station below the courtroom. He took his seat, along with a prison warden.

Justice Charles immediately said, "Do you have council to defend you?"

"No." Replied Pickering.

"I purpose to give you council, your case is one that must be tried. You shall plead not guilty and if you desire, I shall provide you with council to watch over the case for you! Shall I do so?"

Pickering muttered something that was inaudible. The warden sat next to him, stood and said. "The prisoner does not know what to do, he would rather plead guilty."

"Take my advice Pickering." The judge said, "Take your trial, this is the best thing that you can do."

Pickering looked confused as to what was happening and what to do next; he murmured something again to the warden.

The judge told the warden to explain to the prisoner that council would not cost him anything, he needed council to watch the proceedings. The warden said, "He still does not know what to do."

The judge, getting agitated said. "Pickering, take my advice and have a council to watch your case and take your trial. Let that be so. You will take council won't you Pickering?"

There was silence for a moment, Pickering whispered to the warden, he stood up again and said. "He still doesn't know what to do!"

The judge asked the usher to bring in to the court Mr. G. Taylor. He walked into the court, the judge said, "Mr. Taylor, I instruct you to read the dispositions of this case and watch over the proceedings on behalf of the prisoner." Mr. Taylor agreed and sat down to read and familiarise himself with the case.

The prosecution stood and addressed the jury. "The prisoner and the deceased, Jane Pickering had been married for only 3 short months before she died. They lived with the prisoner's mother and father at Czar Street, Holbeck, on the outskirts of Leeds. Pickering was an out of work mechanic, his wife, the deceased, was a weaver at a local mill."

"On the afternoon of the 23rd April 1892, the prisoner, his wife, parents and other members of the family were having tea at the house. Jane after finishing eating took a bowl of water upstairs so she could get washed and changed. Shortly afterwards Pickering went after her. A scream shortly followed, Thomas Pickering ran upstairs to investigate, as he got to the top of the stairs, Jane came out of the bedroom with blood rushing from a wound to her throat. Pickering was laid on his bed, holding a knife. Thomas laid the woman down on the floor and rushed out to get a medical man and the police."

"He came back to the house with the doctor. It was too late to save Jane; her wounds were so severe that she died. In the meantime, Pickering had left the house and was trying to escape. Neighbours and the other occupants of the house were looking for him. In fact a large group of people were hunting him down.

Pickering knowing that he would be spotted in the Street ran in to the back yard of a house and hid in the outhouse. Not long after he was apprehended by the police who were searching the area, and charged with the murder."

The prosecution called Thomas Pickering to the stand.

The crimes behind the hangings

"Henry had not worked since he got married. Jane came home around dinnertime on that day, Henry was still in bed, she wasn't happy at that. We were having family round for tea that day so she said nothing to him, she helped to prepare tea for the family gathering."

Pickering interrupted. "Cut it short!"

Thomas went on, "She went upstairs after tea, and Henry followed 8 or 10 minutes later. Not long afterwards, she screamed. I rushed upstairs; she was coming out of the bedroom with a bad cut to her throat. I grabbed Henry but he said he would not do it again, so I went to fetch Dr. Moore. When I came back Henry had disappeared and Jane died very shortly afterwards."

Mr. Taylor in his cross examination, "What kind of man was your son?"

"He was a quiet man, didn't have much to say, and kept himself to himself, he was trying to find work, but it was difficult." Came the reply.

"How would you describe Jane Pickering?"

"She was very bad tempered and always seemed to be picking on him."

Police constable Wrightson was then called to give evidence.

"I arrived at the house in Czar Street, Dr. Cross was there, the victim had died, after finding out what had happened, I went to try and find Pickering. There was a large crown looking for him, we searched all the gardens, yards, woods etc in the local area.

Eventually he was found in an outhouse in a back yard. I arrested him and he said to me 'Is she dead?' I placed him in irons and took him to the police station. In interview he told me that 'She was going to leave him for someone else, he wasn't going to have that. If he couldn't have her then nobody would. It was all through jealousy."

The owner of a hardware store was called to the stand. "I have a shop in Vicar Lane, in the centre of Leeds. The prisoner came in a couple of days before the 23rd April to buy a bread knife. He asked if it was sharp enough to use straight away."

Mr. Thomas showed the man the knife that had traces of blood on the blade and said. "Is this the knife which you sold Pickering?" "Yes sir!" Came the reply. Mr. Thomas showed the knife to the jury. "This is the knife that was found in the bedroom where the murder was committed. As you can see it had traces of blood on it. The doctor, in his report believed that this is the knife that killed Jane Pickering, nearly severing her head."

The defence didn't have a case to put to the jury. The only thing that Mr. Taylor could do on the prisoner's behalf was to try and get the sentence reduced to manslaughter on the grounds of provocation. This was an impossible task. The jury after deliberating for a short while found the prisoner guilty of murder.

The judge asked Pickering if he had anything to say before sentence was passed. Pickering stood and said. "I have nothing to say except sorry."

The Judge said. "The jury has found you guilty of murder, the evidence pointed to that conclusion and that conclusion only. I will not say a word to aggravate the situation that you are faced with now. I urge you to repent the dreadful crime you have committed in the short time that you have left." He then passed the death sentence in the usual way.

Pickering was taken away and hanged at Armley jail by James Billington on the 14th June 1892.

Chapter 26 – Battered To Death

Moses Cudworth aged 40 and his wife Eliza, along with their 4 children, Mary Alice 18, John Willie 14, James 9 and Katie 4, lived in a three story house in the village of Earby near Keighley. Moses, his wife and eldest daughter all worked at the local mill as weavers, working conditions were strict. Mary Alice lost her job due being absent from work on numerous occasions because of illness.

Cudworth was livid with the girl, as they could not afford the loss of her wages. Eliza had to come to Mary Alice's defence on more than one occasion, as she was afraid that Cudworth would strike the girl.

Mid 1891, James Fylon, Eliza's brother in law, also got work at the same mill as the Cudworth's and he moved his wife and 2 children into Cudworth's house. This put more strain on the family, four adults and 6 children living in a 4 bedroom back to back house.

Eliza had one afternoon off work a week, so she could spend this at home baking bread and buns. But more often than not she would spend this drinking, Cudworth would come home and find his wife passed out, the bread burnt in the oven. This undoubtedly led to arguments sometimes leading to Cudworth taking his hand to Eliza.

In early 1892, Mary Alice managed again to get employment at the mill, but this was short lived as she again lost the job due to her on going illness. The Fylon's had also managed to find accommodation in the village and moved out.

The family could barely make ends meet so they decided that they would take in a lodger. They knew a young man who that had just started work at the mill and was looking for accommodation so they took him in. Once he had moved in, he started taking a more than friendly interest in Eliza.

Cudworth spoke to a neighbour and fellow workmate about this saying. "She sets the table with him sat next to her, I have moved the places around when she is not watching but she always changes them back again without saying owt." "Is that all?" His friend John Booth commented.

Cudworth replied, "He once ordered me to bed one night, so as to be on his own with Eliza. You know he once went away with grocer's wife and he might do the same with mine."

John's advice to this was, "If I were you I'd make him move out. You don't need to have any lodgers; you can do without them."

Cudworth took his friends advice and the lodger was made to leave, though only after some furious arguments between him and his wife.

Throughout the middle of 1892, Eliza kept at him about his jealousy, more arguments than ever before were heard between the couple. Moses started drinking heavier; he wouldn't let Eliza out of his sight, making her go with him wherever he went.

On the Friday 3rd June, they headed down to the White Lion public house, just round the corner from their house, with the Fylon's. The landlord heard a disturbance and found the Fylon's having a violent argument, they were ejected.

On coming back into the pub Matthew Gaunt the landlord, heard another argument and found Eliza on the floor with Moses stood over her, thrashing her. He attempted to eject the Cudworth's but Moses attacked him, however two customers came to Matthew's aid and helped him throw them out of the pub. He was immediately barred from entering the premises again.

That night Moses slept was a knife under his pillow, Eliza spotted it in the morning and asked him what it was there for. His reply was that he had been cutting tobacco with it. They went to work that morning at 6am and as it was Saturday they finished at lunchtime.

The crimes behind the hangings

Moses came home and sent young Willie to the public house to get 2 pints of ale, this didn't last long, so he asked Eliza for some more money. She refused to give him any, as the money she had left was to buy some clogs for Katie that afternoon, and they needed the rest due to it being a holiday weekend, and they weren't back at work until Tuesday.

Moses was livid he stormed out and went round the John Booth's house, on the table in the kitchen there was a glass of beer, Moses just picked it up and without saying a word, drink it in one. John commented to Mrs. Booth that Moses seemed to be in a strange mood. Moses asked if john had anymore drink, John replied, "No, and I have only 2d left after drinking last night! Have you got any money to put to?" Moses didn't have any money so he left, saying as he reached the door, "I will have when I come back."

He went home to get changed out of his working clothes, his suit was missing again, Eliza must have pawned it again. He was furious, he didn't care about Katie wanting some clogs. All he wanted was some money for beer and he as going to get it. He hunted for her, but she had already set of to buy the clogs, he had no alternative than to go and find her.

It only took a couple of minutes for him to catch her, she was about the cross the moors at the top of the hill in the village. He walked up calmly to her and suggested that it was such a lovely day he would walk with her. He asked her for some money to get some beer but she refused. An argument started and Eliza lashed out at Moses grabbing him by the whiskers and tried to stab him with a pocketknife.

Moses picked up a rock, knocked her to the ground and continued raining blows down on her, only stopping when his 4 year old daughter screamed, "Don't do it daddy!"

Thomas Williamson Cowgill lived at the top of the hill which the Cudworth's had walked past before going out of sight. He was around 65 yards away from the scene of the murder, he had heard the little girl scream, but did nothing. He just continued walking down to the village. He did mention it though to a man called James Metcalf, who ran straight away up the hill and onto the moors looking for the Cudworth's. It didn't take him long to come across Eliza, her head had been beaten, blood was everywhere, every bone in her face was broken and her eyes were completely smashed in. There was nothing that James could do, Eliza wasn't breathing, and she had died a horrific death, so he ran off to find a police constable.

Meanwhile back in the village, Moses had arrived home with Katie, Ellen Fylon his sister in law was in the house and Moses asked where Eliza was, Ellen replied, "You should know, you have brought Katie back home." Moses made no reply he picked up Katie and took her to John Booths house, threw down a florin (10p) and said. "Go fetch me a gallon of beer, let me have as much beer as I can before they come and fetch me, I've killed the wife!" He then went onto explain in detail what had happened.

Mr. and Mrs. Booth couldn't believe what they were hearing and ran up to the Cudworths house shouting, "Where is Liza? Moses says he has murdered her!" Eliza was not at there so the Booths went back to home along with Mary Alice who said to her father when she got to the house, "Where is my mother, what had you done to her?" Moses replied, "Where you'll be if I get to you." Then he made a move to grab her. Mrs. Booth managed to stop him in his tracks.

John Booth took Mary Alice back to her own home and then went back to see Cudworth. Moses was sat down, he seemed quite unconcerned about the deed that he had committed, quietly waiting for the police to arrive and take him away.

P.C. White arrived and put Moses in handcuffs, he couldn't understand why they cuffed him, he said, "Why the cuffs, I would have gone without them, I did the deed, I killed her, I will swing like a man." He was taken away and later charged with the wilful murder of his wife.

Eliza's body was taken away for a post mortem and a search was performed in the area, the stone that was covered in blood and used in the murder was taken away, along with a pocket knife which had blood on it handle.

The trial at the West Riding Assizes at Leeds Town Hall was presided over by Mr. Justice Grantham. Mr. Banks and Mr. Edmondson were to conduct the defence, Moses however didn't have any representation therefore Justice Grantham instructed Mr. Wilberforce to act for the defendant.

The defence had only an hour to prepare and take instructions on the case, when the clerk asked whether Cudworth was guilty or not guilty Cudworth replied in a firm voice, "Not guilty."

Medical evidence showed that Eliza suffered from dislocated bottom jaw, the upper jaw was broken and fractured, the nose bone was completely shattered and caved in. The right eye was pushed downward and backwards, the left eyeball was crushed in and burst, the right cheek was covered in cuts and bruises, not a bone in her face was unbroken. The stone that was used in the attack weighed around 6lbs was 8 inches long, 2 inches thick and 6 inches wide.

Mrs. Fylon was called to give evidence; she was the sister of the deceased. She said, "When I went to the lane to see Eliza's body, there were grey whiskers in her left hand, her face was a mess." She quite understandably broke down, sobbing uncontrollably and rocking back and forth in her chair.

Thomas Cowgill was called to the stand he said, "I did not see any blows being struck, I heard a little girl shout 'don't do it daddy', I saw the man stand up near the little girl, he leaned against the fence. I was in a hurry to go to the village to sell some shoes so I left."

The judge said, "But you heard a little girl scream, didn't that make you think the child or somebody might be injured?"

Cowgill replied, "I never had a thought about it at the time."

The judge, "Well I hope you have not got a mind that can think, to act in that way. It's a disgrace to humanity for a strong man to hear a child cry out like that, sixty-five yards away and not take the trouble to go back. You might have saved the life of this woman!"

The defence said it would not suggest that the prisoner didn't kill his wife, the only question was to the circumstances that made him do it. The parties had quarrelled over money for drink, a struggle took place, and the woman pulled a knife, grabbed the prisoner and tried to stab him. The husband retaliated, picked up a stone and struck her. If this is what occurred then the crime was manslaughter and not murder. There was no motive for the crime; they had been happily married for nearly 20 years.

The judge summed up the case to the jury, saying, "The only question that the jury must decide is whether any evidence showed that crime to be manslaughter."

The jury didn't leave the court, after 4 minutes of deliberation they found the prisoner guilty of murder.

The judge passed sentence in the usual way, the prisoner was then taken away to Armley jail. While waiting for the executioner, Cudworth was visited by 3 of his children, however the eldest refused to visit.

Cudworth was distraught by this, he wrote a heartfelt letter to her, when she received it, she relented and made a visit to the jail. Taking with her a petition that had been signed and was going to be delivered to the Home Secretary. Moses didn't want a reprieve he told her, he didn't want to spend the rest of his life in prison, and the best way was to be hung.

His last day consisted on dictating letters to his friends, he said that drink was at the bottom of it all. He urged them to take a warning by his awful fate and not be led into such habits. He did not fear death; he rather welcomed it as a relief from the terrible suffering of the mind he was enduring.

The petition failed, which was a release to Cudworth, he wrote to his family and told them to sell all the possessions and divide the money between the children. Then he waited for the morning of the 18th August.

James Billington arrived at his cell, pinioned him and led him to the gallows. The prison bells were ringing, he climbed the steps to the platform, was then hooded and the noose placed round his neck, Cudworth's last words were, "Lord have mercy on my soul."

Billington pulled the lever; the trap opened and Cudworth dropped. The body was left to hang for the customary hour, then cut down and after a post mortem the body was buried in the confines of the prison, without a coffin, naked except for a shroud, then quicklime was paced over the body.

(Quicklime speeded up the decomposing of the body, and was used after the body of Richard 'Dick' Turpin's had been robbed in 1739, eventually it was recovered and reburied in an unmarked grave, the body covered this time in quicklime).

Chapter 27 – The Hatchet

Edward and Anne Hemmings were married on the 4th June 1892; they lodged at a house in Furnace Lane, Woodhouse, five miles from Sheffield. Mr. Kennington owned the house and they rented a ground floor room, which was used as both the sitting room and the bedroom.

On the 15th February, the had been living in the house for only a matter of 5 weeks, the couple had gone out for a few drinks and arrived back at the house in what was described as on friendly terms. They went to bed, and all was quiet.

At around 3am, George Bradshaw, a fellow lodger at the house was woken by a woman's scream. Bradshaw got out of bed and went to the door of the Hemmings'. He asked if everything was all right, and Hemmings said that it was.

At 4am, Hemmings got up and went off to work as normal. Bradshaw was still concerned about hearing the scream, so he went down and knocked on the door again at about 5am. There was no answer, he tried the handle and the door was unlocked.

He went into the room, and saw straight away Anne laid on the bed. The bedclothes were saturated with blood, Anne had a large cut to her head, and her throat had been cut from ear to ear. It was obvious to Bradshaw that Anne was quite dead. He woke everyone in the house up, he alerted the police and the local doctor.

The police and doctor arrived, the doctor confirmed that Anne had her throat cut by a razor, but previous to that, she had been attacked with what looked like it could have been a hatchet, and she had a fractured skull.

The police set off to search for Hemmings, they searched the local area, in a gulley not far from the house, the found a hatchet, this was identified as belonging to the landlord, and it was covered in blood. A razor was then found it belonged to the prisoner and was also covered in blood. But there was no sign of Hemmings at all. They went to the coal mine where he worked; he had not turned up for work that morning. The scoured, the immediate area, and called in reinforcements to widen the search.

Meanwhile Hemmings it was alleged by some reports that he went to Doncaster and stayed for the night, then he headed of the Normanton, where he had relatives.

He went to at Mrs. Fox's home; he had previously lodged with her and was on quite friendly terms with her. Mrs. Fox knew about the murder when Hemmings arrived at her house.

She said, "I didn't expect to see you again! I thought you might have drowned yourself."

"I think too much of myself to do that." He replied. "I have just come back to see my mates. It's a weight from the head now, I have been suffering for 3 or 4 weeks, now I feel much better, I did love the ground she walked on you know."

Mrs. Fox asked him what had happened and why he had killed her.

He replied, "I heard her talking to another lodger in the kitchen, she called me an idle fellow."

Mrs. Fox then went on and to tell him that the best option was to go to the police station and hand himself in. Which is what Hemmings did.

Inspector Turton worked out of the Normanton police station. Hemmings was waiting for him when he arrived back into the station.

He said to Hemmings, "Hi Ted, what are you doing here?"

"I am here to give myself up, I don't regret what I have done, I planned it for a couple of weeks. I will walk the scaffold like a man."

Turton had just come on duty and had no idea what Hemmings was on about, he went into the back room and spoke to Superintendent Belby, who immediately went and arrested Hemmings for the wilful murder of his wife.

Hemmings said. "If ever a man loved a woman, I loved her. She had a bad temper at times, I just struck her, didn't mean to kill her at the time, I knew that I would get 5 years for it, so I finished off the job. I have no regrets for doing it."

The trail was held at Leeds Assizes on the 15th March 1893. Mr. Justice Gainsford Bruce presided, Mr. Bairstow and Mr. Dodd prosecuted and Mr. Walter Beverley defended Hemmings. The courtroom was packed with reporters, and family and friends of Hemmings.

Mr. Dodd said, "Hemmings was jealous of another lodger in previous lodgings and made threats to harm her on previous occasions. They moved to Woodhouse and he became jealous again of a man living in those lodgings aswell. He had also pulled his knife to Mr. William Jones, telling him that he would do her, as she was always defiant of him."

Mr. Bairstow addressed the jury on the prisoner's behalf. He said. "There was no dispute that the prisoner had killed his wife. The killing was not premeditated, the threats that he had made to his wife, were made over 3 months ago and were not relevant. Something that Anne had said in bed that night, something that they did not know about, caused a serious argument. The prisoner through a moment of madness yielded by a sudden impulse took hold of the weapon, the hatchet and struck her. The jury can only find the prisoner guilty of manslaughter."

The courtroom erupted in cheers and applause to his speech; the officials immediately stopped the disruption.

The jury retired to consider the verdict and returned 40 minute's later finding Hemmings guilty of murder. They recommendation mercy to the prisoner due to provocation.

The judge asked Hemmings if he had anything to say before sentence was passed. He stood and made a long statement about the relations between his wife and another man.

The judge after Hemmings had finished said. "The recommendation for mercy will be passed on to the proper quarter. The evidence proved you, Hemmings have been found guilty of the most cruel and brutal murder. You had with heartless violence taken the life of a woman whom you were bound by every obligation to succour and protect." He then passed the death sentence in the usual way.

Before 26 year old Hemmings was led back down to the cells, he shook hands with Mr. Beverley and thanked him with all his heart; for all that he had done on his behalf. He was taken away to Armley jail, the reprieve was not forthcoming so James Billington executed him on the morning of the 4th April 1893.

Chapter 28 – Low Meadows

Army sergeant Phillip Garner aged 49 was stationed in Belfast in 1875 where he met his wife Agnes and they got married. When he was discharged from the Army they went to live in Liverpool for a while, and then onto Doncaster the town where he was born.

They did not have any accommodation in Doncaster and where living in lodging house. On November 25th 1893 Garner knocked on the door of a Michael Cole enquiring if he had any rooms. Michael didn't but to go and try Mr. Hoyle's which was just down the street. Mr. Hoyle had vacancies and the Garner's moved their few belongings in.

The couple had a few drinks on the Saturday night and they seemed to be on friendly terms. The next morning Garner went out to get some food for breakfast ate it in their room and at around 12.30pm he wanted to go to the pub for a while. Agnes when with him, but it seemed to Mr. Hoyle that she was going under protest.

The couple went to the Lord Nelson, had drinks and then left going in the direction of Low Pastures. When they got to a field at Low Pastures, they both walked down the field, when he thought that they were out of sight, Garner pulled a hammer from his pocket and beat his wife around the head. He threw the badly battered body into a ditch, cleaned the blood from his shoes and calmly walked away.

Two young boys, were playing in a nearby field, they saw him rising out of the ditch and walk out of the field, they were a little curious, so they went for a look. When they got to the ditch, they saw Agnes laid face down and blood everywhere. They ran off to get help.

Mr. Swan was walking the area at the time with his dog. He stumbled across Agnes; he picked her up from the ditch and laid her down conformably in the field. He covered her with his coat, and summed for help. Agnes was taken to the Doncaster Royal Infirmary, where she later died through her brutal injuries. Garner, had left the field and walked calmly to the local police station. He enquired to the constable on the desk if Low Meadows was in his district, The constable confirmed that it was.

Garner said. "My wife is dead!"

The policeman, being a little confused said, "How dead? What do you mean?"

Garner, "My wife is dead there, I have killed her with a hammer! I have knocked her head in. I have tried before to do it before but failed. I have done it this time, look at my hands, and see blood! I left the hammer at her side in the ditch."

The constable called for his sergeant to come through to the front desk.

Garner continued, "I have not lived for years, she was on the streets keeping company with another man. I could not hold it any longer, so I brought her here to kill her. I have done what I intended to do, now I will pay the price."

He was then charged with the murder and remanded in custody by the magistrate's court until his trial at Leeds Assizes.

Mr. Justice Vaughan Williams was sitting at the Leeds Assizes, when Garner first appeared for his trial. After reading the dispositions and consulting with the barristers, Justice Williams ordered that Garner be examined by experts to determine his mental condition. The trial was adjourned until the next Assizes.

Garner was examined by the doctors and was certified to be sane. Therefore he could stand trial for wilful murder.

Justice Williams was not available at the next Assizes in Leeds so the case was presided over by Mr. Justice Collins. Mr. Turton prosecuted and Mr. Lloyd defended the prisoner.

Mr. Turton said that, "The case was as clear as can be, the prisoner admitted the crime, he has been examined by medical men and found to be sane, therefore however painful it is for the jury to convict the prisoner, they must find him guilty of murder."

Mr. Lloyd said, "The jury must find the prisoner guilty of manslaughter, that's if they found a verdict at all. There was sufficient evidence that the prisoner had been drinking and that the deceased had been with another man. Agnes had also been drinking heavily over the previous few weeks and had provoked the prisoner into this crime."

The jury wasted no time in find Garner guilty of murder, the death sentence was passed in the usual way and he was taken away to Armley jail.

James Billington executed him on the 3rd April 1894.

Chapter 29 – Baby Poisoner

Alfred Dews an Iron moulder, lived in the outskirts of Wakefield with his wife and two children. He was a good husband, and a good father that was until the birth of their second child Benjamin.

For some reason, which was not apparent, Dews was under the impression that he did not father the newborn child. This led him to treat his loving wife with cruelty, causing constant arguments and on occasion's violence.

He would also spurn his responsibility of being a father to the young baby, but he showered his eldest child with love and affection.

Dews, in early May was in constant agony, with toothache, he approached a friend who offered him a small bottle which contained a solution consisting of an amount of Ammonia. This friend had told him, that it was poisonous, but in small amounts it would relieve the pain.

Not long after he had received the bottle of liquid, another friend who was visiting Dews at his house, complained of having a bad headache. Dews went and got the small bottle and offered it to them, saying, "Try this, be careful that you don't take too much as it is poisonous."

On the 12th May 1894 Dews was at home looking after the baby, his wife and eldest child had gone out to do an errand. Dews was in the company of a young girl, the daughter of a neighbour, she was called Eliza Hobson. Benjamin was sleeping, nice and quiet, Dews sent the girl away to go and collect something for him.

When she came back a short while later, the baby was very ill, he was vomiting constantly and his mouth and throat was red, raw and inflamed.

Eliza was worried about the child's condition and she asked Dews what he had given him. Dews replied that he hadn't given the child anything, and if she ever mentioned to anyone that he had done so, he would murder her. Eliza insisted that a doctor was called but Dews refused to seek medical assistance.

Benjamin Dews died 11 days later on the 23rd May. Eliza spoke to her parents about what had happened on the night of the 12th May, the police were called and Dews was arrested.

A search was performed at the house of the prisoner, the bottle of poison was found, and it was clear that there was far less liquid in the bottle than there was when Eliza had left to run the errand for Dews.

A post mortem was carried out, but no trace of any poison was discovered. According to the doctor who had conducted the post mortem, it would have been very unlikely for any poison to have been found in the body, due to the length of time it had been between administration and the death. The damage to the baby's health would have been caused almost instantly after consumption.

Dews was charged with murder and appeared at the Assizes at Leeds before Mr. Justice Grantham, Mr. Waddy and Mr. Turton prosecuted the case and Mr. Wilberforce defended Dews.

The defence stated that even if Dews did administer the poison to the child, it was not done with any felonious intent.

The jury after a short deliberation found Alfred Dews guilty of murder, with a strong recommendation of mercy.

The learned judge sentenced Dews to the death sentence and assured the court that he would pass on the recommendation of mercy to the proper quarters.

Dews aged 28 protested his innocence right up to the bolt of the trap being removed by James Billington and him meeting his death. In a letter that he wrote to his wife, he instructed her how to dispose of his property.

Chapter 30 – Helmsley Holiday

Nottingham salesman Robert Hudson aged 23, his wife of 18 months and their baby son came to Helmsley, North Yorkshire, in May 1895 for a holiday, booking into a guesthouse owned by Mrs. Holmes.

Hudson was quite familiar with the area as he was born in Helmsley and had lived his early life in and around the Village, he still had family living close by, which the couple were planning on visiting.

Immediately on arrival, the couple and child were intent on going for long walks over the moors, which were quite close to the village. It seemed to all that they were a happy, content and affectionate couple, enjoying the countryside and fresh air.

On the 5th June Hudson purchased a spade from a man in Helmsley called Edwin Trenham and strapped it to the bicycle that he had brought up from Nottingham with him. He rode off on his bike at about noon that day towards the moors. A couple of hours later, he was seen riding back into Helmsley but without the spade.

The next day and gentleman by the name of Mr. Tyreman was walking on the moors, when under some trees he noticed a freshly dug hole, which appeared to be empty.

8th June, around 9am before leaving the guesthouse, Hudson ordered dinner for himself and his family for the usual time. The three of them set off again towards the moors, heading in the same direction which Hudson was seen coming back from 3 days previous, and where the freshly dug hole which Mr. Tyreman had come across was.

At about 1.45pm Hudson was seen coming back into the village, from the direction that he had gone earlier, this time he was alone. A witness who had seen him coming into the village later gave a statement saying that Hudson looked agitated and his hands were twitching.

He arrived at the guesthouse around 2pm, Mrs. Holmes was not in at the time and Hudson went straight to his room.

When Mrs. Holmes arrived back home she was surprised to see Hudson without his wife and child, asking where they were, Hudson replied that they had gone that afternoon to see his blind Aunt Wilsons who lived in Hovingham. His cousins Lizzie and Ernest were also there and wanted them to stay over for a few days. He had come back to collect a few clothes; he was catching the 3.30pm train to Hovingham that afternoon and they were staying until Monday when they would be back at the guesthouse.

On cleaning Hudson's room the next morning, Mrs. Holmes noticed in the sink, a small amount of grit and dirt, also Hudson had taken all his belongings with him leaving his wife and child's clothes there.

In fact Hudson did not get the 3.30pm train to Hovingham, he took a train straight back to Nottingham. He wrote to Mrs. Holmes on the 10th June asking if she would send the belongings to the address that he gave.

He also wrote on the same day to a Mrs. Robinson who lived in Sheffield and was one of his wife's sisters. In the letter it said "Kitty, my beloved wife has left me, and worse than that she has taken the child with her, leaving a note saying she could not live with me, and that she had been unhappy. She left me with little or no money and I don't know what will become of her. I have commenced a search for her and I don't intend to give up. I don't know if she has gone with anyone but I suspect it."

The police were called and a search was instigated to find the missing mother and child. While searching the moors near Helmsley on the 16th June, the bodies were discovered buried at the exact spot that Mr. Tyreman had seen the freshly dug hole. A carving knife was found in the make shift grave, Mrs. Hudson was terribly cut, her jugular vein was severed and a bullet was lodged in her head.

The very next day Robert Hudson was arrested in Birmingham, in the case that he was carrying, was a carving fork and sharpening steel, matching the carving knife, which the police had recovered. He was also in procession of a revolver, a bullet missing from the chamber and of the same calibre which was found lodged in the skull of Kate Hudson.

His notebook had a strange entry dated 15th June, 1895 written in Hudson's own handwriting it said, "1 week from the saddest event of my life, at 10 minutes to 1 and I am still living." Hudson was charged with the wilful murder of his child and baby son and appeared in the York Assizes before Mr. Justice Matthew on the 23rd July 1895.

The prosecution, Mr. Waddy Q.C. and Mr. F.D. Blake had a watertight case, they had the revolver, the knife, they also had the spade which was found on the 21st June, 200 yards away from the burial, hid in a patch of heather. They also had a copy of a newspaper advertisement, which Hudson had placed, which read 'Bachelor, tall, dark, aged mid twenties, wishes to meet with a lady of some means with a view to early marriage, Honourable and sympathetic'.

Dr. Hingston, medical Superintendent of the North Riding of Yorkshire Lunatic Asylum, Dr. Hitchcock and Dr. Tempest Anderson, the medical Superintendent and the consulting physician of the York Lunatic Asylum respectively all gave evidence for the crown. Each stating that in their opinion Hudson was of sound mind at the time in question.

Mr. Wragge who represented the prisoner said, "The prisoner and his wife lived together on the happiest of terms." He continued "He had always borne the highest of character, the facts which the prosecution have given to the court are not contested, the only question which the jury have to decide is whether Hudson was sane at the time of the alleged murder or not".

Medical evidence on behalf of the defendant showed that for first 14 years of his life, he was in extremely poor health. Since that time he had suffered from pains at the back of the head.

Dr. Oglesby, medical officer of the York Union was called to give medical evidence on behalf of the defendant, as was Dr. Bevan Lewis, the medical superintendent of the Wakefield Asylum. Dr. Bevan was pushed to answer a question put to him directly by the learned judge, his reply was. "The prisoner would know that cutting his wife's throat would kill her and that it was the wrong thing to do."

The jury retired at 5pm, after only 8 minutes they returned to the court with a verdict of guilty.

The prosecution then stood and offered no evidence in the charge of the murder of Heseltine Hudson, the prisoner's son.

Sentence of death was passed in the usual way, Mr. Justice Matthew added that the prisoner must be prepared to follow his victims. He was taken to York castle jail and executed on the 13th August 1895 by James Billington.

Chapter 31 – A Shilling

Irish born labourer Patrick Morley aged 38 and his wife lived in Batley an area near Dewsbury in West Yorkshire. The marriage was an unhappy one, with Morley constantly drinking and abusing Elizabeth both verbally and physical threats were often made towards her. Many times over the recent months and years, Elizabeth had either thrown Morley out of the marital home or she left, but always returning a few days later.

The arguments continued and so did the physical threats of violence she suffered by Morley. On two separate occasions the police were called to the house, Morley arrested and then brought before the Magistrates Court where he was bound over to keep the peace.

Around the 3rd September 1895 Morley had been out drinking and came home and started fighting with his wife, he brutally assaulted her, therefore the next morning Elizabeth packed her belongings and moved out. She lodged with a Mrs. Nutton also living in Batley, determined that she was not going back to the marital home again.

Morley kept his distance for the first few weeks of their separation apparently working hard and staying away from the drink. Hoping that if he changed Elizabeth would come back home again. On the morning of September 22nd he visited Mrs. Nutton and asked if he could speak to Elizabeth.

Apparently according to Mrs. Nutton, Elizabeth was not at home, she had gone to Mass at the local church. Morley left the house saying that he would return later that day.

He called back at the house at around 1pm; Elizabeth was in the kitchen cutting some parsley for dinner, Morley said, "Elizabeth can you lend me a shilling?" Elizabeth replied. "You know Pat, I haven't a shilling to lend you. I have been playing over the holidays just like you, I have not got my piece work money, and I wont get any money till the mill re-opens."

Morley replied. "Get away Elizabeth." He then pulled a revolver from his inside pocket and fired it at Elizabeth. The bullet hit her in her right temple; she fell to the ground and died not long afterwards. Morley turned the gun towards his own mouth and pulled the trigger. His hand was shaking, and unfortunately the bullet missed, lodging itself in the kitchen wall.

He turned round said, "I have done what I intended to do." then he ran out of the kitchen and down the street.

Mrs. Nutton managed to summon a police constable and Morley was arrested not far away from the house where the murder was committed. He was brought back to the house, while they waited for transport to take him to the police station.

A doctor was examining the body, he certified that Elizabeth was dead, Morley said, "I am sorry, I hope her soul is in heaven." Adding, "I did if for love."

Morley appeared at the Leeds Assizes on the 9th December 1895, in front of Mr. Justice Grantham, Mr. Harold Thomas led the prosecution, Mr. Bromet conducted the defence.

The prisoner pleaded insanity, his defence barrister said, "The prisoner is addicted to drink and at the time of the shooting of his wife, he looked wild and acted very strange."

The prosecution said, "The crime was committed because the victim refused to move back to her husband nor would she lend him a shilling. He pulled out his revolver and shot her in cold blood."

The learned judge summed up the evidence of case to the jury, the evidence he said, "Weighed heavily in favour of the prosecution."

The jury did not leave the bench to deliberate the verdict; they found the prisoner guilty of wilful murder. Mr. Justice Grantham asked Morley if he had anything to say before sentence was passed, Morley replied, "At the time I was weak in the head, I am ready to be examined by a doctor. I loved my wife and had no intention of killing her, I only took out the revolver to frighten her and I had now idea that it would go off. If Elizabeth had given me a shilling I would not have had any cause to pull out the revolver."

Morley was given the death sentence in the normal way, then was taken to the condemned cell at Armley jail where he waited 22 days before he was executed by James Billington on new years eve 1895.

Chapter 32 - The Sailor

Joseph Robert Ellis aged 22 a sailor had been married for 15 months to Emma Ellis also aged 22. The relationship broke down after Emma had given birth to their child, Ellis had frequently threatened to take her life, so Emma moved back to live with her parents in Clegg's Yard, Goole.

On June 24th 1886 the couple executed a deed of separation and Ellis was ordered to pay 5 shillings week maintenance for Emma and the upkeep of the young child.

July 1st 1896, Ellis travelled to Clegg's Yard with a piece of paper that he wanted Emma to sign in receipt for the 5s that he had previously sent to her. Emma was in the act of signing the paper when Ellis grabbed her by the neck with his left hand and stabbed her twice in the left side with a knife, which he was holding in his right hand. Emma rushed out of the house closely followed by her mother to neighbours.

On the way back to their house Ellis came up behind her and stabbed her a couple of times again to her left side. It was these blows that made Emma crash to the floor.

Ellis continued stabbing Emma with such frenzy that he only stopped when the handle of the knife broke off. Emma was rushed to the Cottage Hospital, Goole; she was in a critical condition and the following morning she died from her injuries.

Joseph Ellis was later seen the same day of the attack in a street in Goole attempting to cut his throat with another knife, he was stopped from doing so and was also taken to the Cottage Hospital.

Dr. Grainger Brown who treated his neck wound attended the prisoner. He had previously treated him a couple of days before the attack for infection of the eyes, the doctor was to state that it was probable that the prisoner was at the time he attacked his wife was suffering from 'impulsive insanity'.

While the prisoner was detained overnight at the Cottage Hospital, he suffered from a convulsive attack, another doctor had to be called for to treat Ellis.

Ellis was charged with the murder of his wife Emma and was sent for trial at the Assizes at Leeds Crown Court, August 1896.

Mr. Banks and Mr. Whitaker appeared for the prosecution and Mr. C. Mellor represented Ellis.

Mr. Mellor for the defence addressed the jury saying. "He did not ask them to come to the conclusion that Ellis was insane at the time he attacked his wife, but he contended that the circumstances were such that would justify them in finding the prisoner guilty of the lesser charge of manslaughter.

The jury retired to consider the verdict and when they returned the found the prisoner Joseph Robert Ellis guilty of murder.

Mr. Justice Kennedy passed sentence of death in the usual way. James Billington executed Ellis on the 25th August 1896 at Armley jail.

Chapter 33 – Swedish Sailor

Swedish born August Carlsen a 43 year old seaman worked on a fishing boat that was based in the port of Hull, he would always take his shore leave in the town and not return to his home country. While on shore leave previous to 1896 he met a woman called Julia Wood aged 38 and eventually whenever the boat docked in Hull Carlsen would spend his time with Julia.

They were on very affectionate terms; Carlsen would always give Julia plenty of money to live on while he was away. But if Julia ran out of money she turned to her part time job, prostitution. Carlsen knew about this, he wasn't happy at all and on many occasions he would beat Julia over it.

Julia wrote many letters to him expressing her true love and affection that she had for him, missing him all the time he was aboard ship, she always signed the notes Florrie - the pet name which Carlsen had for her.

Julia lodged at a house in Hull belonging to Mrs. McCann; her bedroom was the front room on the ground floor, whenever Carlsen was in Hull he would stay with Julia.

Carlsen had shore leave in the middle of July 1896, he arrived as normal to be with Julia, spending most of the time between July 18th and the 22nd frequenting the public houses in the area, returning back to the lodgings both well under the influence of drink.

On the night of 22nd July they returned home, and had an argument that led to Carlsen assaulting Julia, causing her to have swollen lips and black eyes.

The next day neither Carlsen or Julia left their room, they had asked a fellow lodger to bring some beer to the house for them, the lodger did so and throughout the day the couple consumed 4 shillings worth of brandy, 2 pints of ale and 2 bottles of ale. At 7.30pm that evening Carlsen approached the landlady and said, "I have killed Florrie, I have cut her throat go for a policeman."

The crimes behind the hangings

Mrs. McCann sent immediately for a policeman and a doctor, when they arrived at the house and went into the bedroom. Carlsen was laid on the bed with his arms around Julia, he was asked twice to get up but failed to respond, as if he didn't understand or was under the influence of drink.

Carlson kept repeating, "I'm willing to die – I'm ready to die for her any minute."

The policeman managed to move Carlsen from the bed so the doctor could examine Julia. The doctor found a 6" long wound to Julia's neck, the blood stained razor that was laid in the bed next to Julia had caused it. The doctor ascertained that death would have been almost instantaneous. Carlsen was arrested and charged with the murder of Julia Wood.

The trial was held at York Assizes, the presiding judge was Mr. Justice Grantham, Mr. Harold Thomas and Mr. Edmondson represented to treasury.

The defence urged that the prisoner was drunk when for some reason he decided it was necessary to commit the act. In the circumstances the jury would be justified in the finding Carlsen guilty of manslaughter, there was evidence that the woman had treated him badly and he had been provoked into the attack.

The jury retired and returned to the court 45 minutes later, they found the prisoner guilty of the murder of Julia Wood, with a strong recommendation of mercy. His lordship donned the black cap and passed sentence of death on the prisoner, adding that the recommendation for mercy shall be passed on the proper quarter.

Carlsen was taken away and hanged at Hull prison on the 22nd December 1896 by James Billington.

Chapter 34 – Family Robinson

Sarah Pickles lived in Green Lane, Thornton, near Bradford with her son William; she also had an elderly couple living with her. The man being 73 years old, and the woman being 72. Sarah was married but she lived apart from her husband. She had taken her cousin in as a lodger who worked as a wool comber in the area. He lived with them from October 1986 until April 1897.

Robinson often came home drunk and became argumentative, disrupting the rest of the house. He didn't like other lodgers staying at the house, in particular a young female lodger who often had her boyfriend staying over. He many times commented that the house was being run immorally. Sarah asked him to leave, which he did without too much trouble. Robinson moved to School Green, Thornton, but he would often still visit the house.

On the 10th June 1897, Robinson came round to the house, after he had been drinking, an argument started between Sarah and Robinson with resulted in Sarah receiving a black eye. He was asked to leave but he wouldn't go, he started pushing her and shouting. William was home at the time. He was upstairs, when he heard all the commotion going on in the kitchen he came downstairs to assist his mother. Eventually they managed to get Robinson out of the house, his last comments to the couple were that he would kill her and she won't be able to hide behind her son forever.

Sarah was livid; she was not going to put up with this behaviour anymore. So she marched straight round to the police station and made a statement to them. The police issued a summons for Robinson to appear at court for using threatening language. This was served on him on the 11th June.

Robinson showed a friend Arthur Horsfall the summons, he denied all the allegations and said that he would get the summons withdrawn, but if he went to jail he would kill her as soon as he was released. After work that day he went round to see Mrs. Pickles to sort out the matter.

The crimes behind the hangings

Robinson was seen by 2 people that evening walking directly to Sarah's door and walking in. He immediately locked the door and went into the kitchen. Sarah was there, but her son was out.

She said. "Have you come about the summons? Let's settle it."

Robinson said. "I'll settle it." And then grabbed her round the throat, he pulled out a razor and slit her windpipe, before hacking the body a few times. When he was finished he unlocked the door, went out, locked the door behind him, and went home.

The frail old lady in the house was powerless to help, she saw him come in the kitchen and heard what was happening. As soon as Richardson left, she went to summon the police.

The police and a doctor came to the house, Sarah was pronounced dead and was taken away for a post mortem, then the police searched the house. They found that Robinson had left his razor, a knife and his cap behind at the scene of the murder. They waited until the morning before going to arrest Robinson.

Police constable Hesselwood arrested him Robinson the next morning, when he told him what he wanted him for Robinson said.

"Sarah is at home, she is alright."

Hesselwood replied. "No she's not, the doctor says that she is dead."

"Yes, that's what I mean, I am now satisfied, I have had my revenge. If it had not been for the summons I would not of done it." Replied Robinson.

Robinson was charged with the murder and later appeared at the Assizes in Leeds on the 30th June in front of Mr. Justice Wright. Mr. Banks and Mr. Brent Grotrian appeared for the prosecution and Mr. Walter Beverley and Mr. Newell represented Robinson.

Robinson was dressed in a black suit, white shirt and a green tie when he stood and replied to the clerk that he was not guilty. The prosecution called the old couple, and the other witnesses that saw Robinson go in to the house that evening. They called Mr. William Pickles, Sarah's son who gave evidence of what it was like to share a house with Robinson.

William Pickles was also asked whether he knew about the insanity which ran in the family, 2 or 3 of the Robinson family were alleged to be in an asylum, and also 2 relatives had committed suicide by slitting there throats. William said that he knew nothing about these members of the family.

The defence said that, "Was it not for a reasonable inference from the evidence, that in doing what he did, something must have taken possession of his mind and he became unaccountable for his actions. It was shown that madness was in the family and 2 persons from the same family were in an institution."

His lordship said, "I am bound to tell the jury that I can not see nothing to support the theory of insanity."

The jury agreed with Mr. Justice Wright. They found the prisoner guilty of murder. The sentence of death was passed in the usual way. James Billington executed Robinson aged 32, on the 17th August 1897. His eldest son Thomas Billington assisted him in the double execution at Armley jail. The other man to be executed was a man called Joseph Robinson.

The newspapers picked up on this unusual event, one papers headline was, 'The Billington's execute the Robinson's.'

Chapter 35 – 30 Minute Trial

33 year old Barnsley miner, Joseph Robinson had been married to Florence who was 9 years his junior since 1891. It was a happy marriage at the beginning and the couple had two children. Florence came from a well-respected family, having family values installed on her from very early age. She had married by choice, whilst she was still in her teens. She was determined that her children would be brought up with the same family values. Robinson on the other hand, didn't care; he worked hard and drunk most nights.

Robinson was jealous of his young wife. Neighbours would often hear arguments coming from the house, normally due to his jealousy. The more he drink the more he became jealous, the more jealous he became the more he drunk.

The police had been called to the house on many occasions due to the arguments and the threats that Robinson had made towards his wife. Robinson had been bound over to keep the police on a few occasions. The couple had separated frequently but always got back together for the sake of the kids.

Florence's cousin Mr. Robert Marshall who lived in Claremont, Monk Bretton, between Barnsley and Wakefield, had a disabled wife. She needed round the clock female nursing as she was confined to bed. Robert asked Florence if she would help for a while, he needed to get back to his job as an engine driver, it would only be temporary until he found someone full time.

Florence agreed and spoke to Robinson about it. He was furious, there was no way that he was going to allow her to work away from home, not even for a day. Florence argued that it was family and that she was going. Robinson was fighting a losing battle; Florence was adamant that she was going. She arranged for her mum to look after the children, and made plans to leave the following day.

At the train station, Robinson was still trying to persuade her not to go. He made more threats as to what would happen if she did go. She got on the train and left. Robinson turned round, kissed one of his children goodbye, swore at his mother in law, then disappeared.

Florence got to Claremont and told Robert Marshall what had happened, he advised her to always lock the door when he went to work. This she did for a while through the state of fear she was under.

On the 13th May 1897, Robert left for work at 1.30pm, Florence was busy and didn't lock the door in time, as only a couple of minutes after Robert had gone, the door opened and in walked Robinson. Within a couple of minutes of him being in the house, 2 shots were heard then Florence screamed out, "Joe's shot me." She tried to open the back door, but fell as the 3rd bullet hit her just behind he left ear. She fell dead in the doorway.

Mrs. Marshall heard everything from upstairs; she was helpless to do anything. She couldn't even get out of bed to bang on the window to attract attention.

Neighbours alerted by the sounds of the shots rushed round to the house to find Florence laid dead in the doorway, and Robinson was drinking some fluid out of a bottle. The bottle had a label that said Laudanum (An opium based poison.) and a red cross.

A neighbour had summoned police constable Hanson, when he walked into the house he saw the empty bottle of liquid and Robinson sat on a chair. He immediately went to the sink, found a drinking vessel filled it with water and a mixture of mustard and made Robinson drink it. This made Robinson violently sick, and had undoubtedly saved his life. He was rushed to Beckett's Hospital in Barnsley where he made a full recovery.

Robinson was charged with the murder of his wife and was remanded in custody until the Assizes at Leeds. His case was heard on the 29th July 1897 in front of Mr. Justice Wright.

Mr. Mellor prosecuted Robinson and Mr. Percy Middleton defended him. It was stated in the evidence for the prosecution that Robinson had pawned some of his belongings to enable him to purchase the revolver and the Laudanum.

The defence said that Robinson had no intention of killing his wife, the jury would be justified in finding him guilty of manslaughter only, on the ground that he caused her death by accidental shooting.

The judge said, "There can be do doubt the prisoner took his wife's life and intended to do so. A man went into a house with a revolver and poison and locks the door. There can have no other alternative explanation to explain these actions. The facts are clear and simple. I do not know any other verdict that the jury can be justified in returning, except guilty of murder."

The jury didn't even leave the jury box. They returned the verdict of guilty of murder. The judge passed the sentence of death in the usual way.

From start to finish the trial lasted a record time of 30 minutes. The prisoner was taken to Armley jail to wait for the execution day.

17th August 1897, James Billington and his eldest son pinioned Joseph Robinson in the condemned cell, then he was lead to the gallows, and he stood along side Walter Robinson in what was going to be another double execution at Armley jail.

A statement from the governor of the prison said that the men were not related at all to each other, they had both been model prisoners while in confinement at the jail. Last night quite understandably had been restless for the prisoners, but religion had helped them through the night.

Chapter 36 – 2 Little Girls

Thomas Mellor aged 29, his common law wife Ada Beecroft, and two children lived together in Holbeck, Leeds. Ada was committed to Menston Mental Asylum, where she died in November 1899. Just before her untimely death, Mellor and his two children Ada age 6 and Annie age 4 moved in with another woman called Priscilla Redshaw at No' 6 Fourth Court.

Priscilla had two children of her own, however she sent them to live with her mother so she could devote more time in helping Mellor look after his two young children. Ada, was unwell, she was the oldest of the children, but was the weakest, being admitted to Leeds Infirmary on numerous occasions for medical treatment.

Mellor worked as a labourer making a reasonable amount of money for a single man without children. Unfortunately Mellor was a father with 2 children, had a common law wife and the responsibility of providing a roof over their heads. This was hard enough to do on his wages, but Mellor also enjoyed a good drink and was addicted to horse racing.

Their home, which was sparsely furnished, with many windows broken, was taken from them due to rent arrears. Their few possessions were stored in a nearly disused stable and they would sneak back to the house on an evening to sleep, before having to leave the next morning so they wouldn't get discovered.

On Friday 11th May, Mellor gave Priscilla eight shillings out of his 17 shillings wages, Priscilla was livid and demanded more money to feed the family, Mellor stormed out of the house and went down to the pub. Priscilla followed him with the two children, left the children with him and said that she was leaving him.

He was at a loss as what to do now; he visited his brother Arthur, to ask if he would allow his family to stay with him. Arthur, as much as he would have like to help had no alternative but to say no, there just was not enough room for another 3 people.

His last hope was the Holbeck Guardians Workhouse. He explained the situation to them, however they refused to help on the grounds that they believed that he had enough money to look after himself and the children.

Mellor was now desperate, he had no where to live and two young children to look after, he hinged a plan which would make certain that his two daughters would be taken into care by the authorities.

He walked down the bank of Leeds-Liverpool canal, off Globe road, Holbeck, Leeds and waited. When he saw a man walking towards them, he placed the two children into a shallow part of the canal and ran off, hoping that the children would scream, therefore get rescued and then the girls would be taken in to care.

At 5.30 the next morning a man called William Wilson was walking down the canal, when he spotted a couple of rags floating in the water. The rags unfortunately were the bodies of Ada and Annie Beecroft.

The police were called and the bodies were taken to the mortuary for identification. Thomas Mellor was quickly arrested and charged with murder of his two daughters.

At the trial at West Yorkshire Assizes in Leeds, Mr. Marshall conducted the defence. Said to the jury that a verdict of murder could not be reached as, Mellor had only placed the girls in the canal in the expectation that they would scream, attract attention and be promptly rescued before they would come to any harm. Therefore a verdict of manslaughter was more appropriate.

In summing up the judge said that Mellor was deserving of a little sympathy, he had failed to find somewhere safe for his two children to live, however he did put the two girls in the canal. If his attention was as the defence had suggested, why did he not just leave the girls on a street corner where they would have been found by the police.

The jury adjourned and then returned to the court 17 minutes later, returning the verdict of murder of Annie Beecroft.

In the case of murdering Ada, the prosecution offered no evidence to support the case, so Mellor was found not guilty.

The judge before passing sentence said to Mellor. "You have been convicted, and I think properly of the murder of practically both your children. The jury has recommended mercy, which will be passed onto the proper quarter."

Mellor was removed from the court, distraught taking the news badly. His father and stepmother visited him just before the day of his hanging and found him in poor health and not eating properly. He continued to hope that he would get a reprieve, a petition was signed by several thousand people, but arrived at the Home Secretary's office too late.

James and William Billington executed him on the 16th August 1900 along side Charles Backhouse at Armley jail.

Chapter 37 – P.C. Kew

Brother's Charles Benjamin aged 23 and his younger brother Frederick aged 19, both miners were notoriously well known to the local police at Swinton, Rotherham. In particularly police constable John Kew, had more than his fair share of dealing with these two undesirable characters.

July 1st 1900 and P.C. Kew had again the honour of visiting Frederick Backhouse to issue a warrant to appear at the local court to answer the charge of assault on his brother Charles's wife. The court date was set for July 9th, Frederick did not appear at this hearing and he was fined in his absence 40 shillings plus costs, or in default of non-payment a custodial sentence of 30 days would be imposed.

The two bothers had left Swinton on the 7th July and did not return home until the 10th July where Charles purchased a 6 chambered revolver and nine cartridges from a place about 5 miles from his home.

The Backhouse brother's were then seen the same day brandishing the gun around in public making threats to passers-by. A woman had seen this and had run to P.C Kew to inform him of the incidents.

P.C. Kew no alternative than to visit the Backhouse's and investigate. He arrived at the gateway of their house at no 75 Piccadilly, Swinton, Rotherham, just as the two brothers were about to leave.

He said, "I am entitled to search both of you Charles and Frederick." At the same time reaching out to perform the search on the eldest brother. Charles stepped back, pulled out the revolver and shot P.C. Kew in the stomach.

Even though he had been shot and was in considerable pain, P.C Kew reached for the hand which held the revolver and forced it behind Charles' back saying, "Why have you shot me Charles, I have done you no harm." Charles was to reply, "I have not shot you."

Frederick reached for the revolver from his brother, aimed it again at the wounded policeman and said, "Here is another one for you." Shooting him in the hip.

Even though John Kew was severely wounded he struggled the short distance to his own house where he managed to retell the account of the shooting; He died from his injuries around 2pm the next day.

The Backhouse brothers were arrested, when charged with the murder. Charles reply was, "Yes." Where as Frederick said, "Yes we did it, we were drunk at the time."

The medical evidence in the shooting was that the bullet, which Frederick had administered, was not sufficient in itself to cause death, but the bullet fired by Charles was the fatal bullet.

Mr. Harold Thomas and Mr. Edmondson prosecuting the case, upon hearing the medical evidence, they dropped the charge of murder against Frederick Backhouse and replaced the charge with aiding and abetting in the committing of the offence.

The jury returning the verdicts found both prisoners guilty of the charges against them, but recommended mercy for Frederick due to his age.

The learned judge Mr. Justice Ridley explained that the verdict amounted to a verdict of guilty of murder, the death sentence had to be passed. In the case of Frederick Backhouse the recommendation of mercy would be passed to the proper quarter.

The prisoners were taken to Armley gaol to await the inevitable punishment of hanging. Which had been arranged for August 16th 1900.

Two days before the execution Frederick Backhouse received a reprieve from the Home Secretary, his sentence was reduced to life imprisonment. James Billington hanged his brother along side Thomas Mellor, in the first hanging at Armley goal in the 20th century.

Chapter 39 – Two Trials

Charles Oliver Blewitt aged 33 lived at No 7 Star Fold, Beeston, Leeds, with his wife of 4 years Mary Ann. Blewitt had been out of work for 9 weeks, this brought severe hardship to the household and caused many arguments between to couple. Many neighbours and friends of the couple believed that they had a perfect marriage if it wasn't because of the unemployment. On the 8th June 1900 William Sydney, who lived at No 6 Star Fold heard the couple having another argument. He heard Mary say to Charles, "Just go and find some work." Shortly afterwards he heard the door close. Mr. Roger Coffey the resident of No 8 Star Fold then saw Blewitt walk down the street. Blewitt said something to him that he did not quite hear.

Blewitt now cleaned shaved and smartly dressed was seen early the next morning walking on the road from Leeds towards Halifax. A police constable stopped and asked the man where he was going. He said that his name was Oliver Jackson and was going to find work, the constable allowed him to continue his journey.

Blewitt's mother, Mrs. Bunney had stored a few possessions at the home of her son and had gone round the find the house in complete darkness, the doors and windows locked and the blinds closed. She spoke to the neighbours and they reported that neither of the couple had been seen since Friday evening. Mrs. Bunney was not too alarmed at the time; they might have gone away for the weekend so she decided to try again later in the week.

She went back round again and still got no answer, she was starting to become suspicious. On the 17th June, she went along with her husband James and Mr. Thomas Armitage the landlord, to the house and forced entry by the front door.

They immediately found the body of Mary sat in the rocking chair in the front room. Her head was covered in a shawl, her throat was slit and blood had soaked her clothes and the shawl. The police were called and when they arrived they conducted a search of the property. A butcher's knife was found in the kitchen drawer, the handle had bloodstains on it. A pair of boots that were in the kitchen had blood splat on them and Mary's purse was found near the fireplace, again this had bloodstains on it and was empty. The police concluded that it was impossible for Mary to have slit her throat, put the knife back in the drawer, walked back into the room, sat down and covered her head without blood been splattered all over. Therefore they ruled out suicide. They interviewed the neighbours and it was became certain that Charles Blewitt was the last person to been seen leaving the house and was most definitely the murderer.

The search began for Blewitt; the rumours started spreading as to where he was, some say that he was working at either Barnsley or Sheffield. Others were that he had thrown himself into the local canal. The police believed that he was working in the Yorkshire area and had changed his name.

On the 1st July the police searched the house again, this time it was a more through search, they found the couples wedding certificate, a gun and a note addressed to George Jackson, Mary's brother. It asked him to keep the certificate and a gun until she asked for it back. George said that in his opinion the marriage was struggling.

The local newspapers had got hold of the story and reported the murder along with a description of Blewitt. He was working at a foundry in Halifax when a work mate showed him the newspaper that carried a picture of the wanted man. He asked Jackson if he had been to Beeston. Jackson (Alias Blewitt) said he lived in Morley, he had never been to Beeston but knew where it was.

The workman was still suspicious and reported the matter to the police. The next morning on turning up at work, Jackson was called into the manager's office, the police were waiting for him and he was arrested and taken back to the police station at Leeds for questioning.

He was charged with the murder of his wife and appeared at the Assizes at Leeds on the 30TH July before Mr. Justice Ridley.

Blewitt pleaded not guilty, he said he knew nothing of the murder of his wife and she must have committed suicide. The prosecution was having a hard time in convincing the jury that Blewitt was the murder, they retired to consider the verdict, but came back into the courtroom 30 minutes later.

The foreman addressed the judge and said that it was impossible for them to reach a verdict that they all could agree on.

The judge said that he would accept a majority verdict, again the foreman said it would be impossible for them to even come to a majority.

The learned judge had no alternative than to discharge the jury and he ordered a re-trial, which was set for 7th August.

This time Mr. Justice Bruce presided, the barristers were the same, Mr. W.J.W Wraugh and Mr. C.F Parmer for the defence and Mr. Banks and Mr. Grotian for the prosecution. The courtroom was packed again and Blewitt pleaded not guilty.

Dr. Heald's evidence was that the shawl could not have been placed over Sarah's head herself, in his opinion someone whom obviously she trusted had come up behind her and slit her throat.

There was no blood anywhere other than on the deceased and around the chair she was found in. There were small cuts to her hands suggesting that she tried to defend herself and pointing away from suicide.

Roger Coffey and William Sydney gave evidence as to the last time that they saw Blewitt.

William Sydney said he heard Sarah tell Charles to go and find work, then he heard a sound that sounded like someone had falling down the stairs, closely followed by the door banging.

Mr. Banks on summing up the case to the jury said, "I will leave it to the jury to use their common sense as to whether it was suicide or murder. Assuming it was murder, was it the prisoner or another man? If it was another man there were great difficulties in the case. It must be someone who got into the room as soon as the prisoner left that Friday night, and before supper was cleaned away. It must have been someone whom Sarah had let into the house, as there was no noise, or even marks of anyone attempting to break in. Sarah must have trusted this person as she was grabbed from behind and her windpipe was severed before she reacted. The prisoner disappeared the night of the murder, altered his appearance and changed his name to Jackson. All he took with him was the clothes he was wearing, and a razor. He must have had money with him, and remember his wife's empty purse was found with a bloody fingerprints on it. He left the house on a Friday night was it not strange to go looking for work on a Saturday and Sunday?"

The defence summed up the case as they saw it to the jury, after speaking in great length about the lack of motive Mr. Wraugh went on to say. "Wasn't it strange that a man who had never before been in trouble with the police, would suddenly commit the most atrocious crime known to man. The prisoner's mother and stepfather have given evidence that it was not unusual for the prisoner to shave of his moustache and beard, why wouldn't he smarten himself up, wouldn't it be the natural thing to do as he was going looking for work? He didn't take his possessions with him as he only intended to be away for a short time. When he was in Halifax he never once tried to hide the fact that he was from Leeds."

The judge addressed the court and said, "Due to the time, I think that it would be better for the jury to start their deliberations tomorrow instead of at this hour. This court will adjourned until 10.30am tomorrow."

The next morning, the judge thanked Mr. Wraugh for his most able defence and then addressed the jury to the evidence that they should consider. He finished by saying. "Dismiss any suggestions of suicide. You must be satisfied not only that Sarah was murdered, but that also the prisoner had murdered her."

The jury retired at 1.15pm and came back into the courtroom at 1.57pm. The foreman stood and said they found the prisoner guilty of murder.

His lordship turned to Blewitt and said, "The jury after a careful trial and after hearing the most able defence by your counsel have found you guilty of the crime, which you are charged. I have only to say that I agree with that verdict. You will have an opportunity, which you denied your poor victim, of making preparations for your great change. It only remains for me to pass the sentence of death."

Blewitt was taken away to the condemned cell at Armley jail, not once did he mention what did happen that night to anyone, even though he had visitors before the execution. He walked unassisted to the gallows on the 28th August 1900 and was executed by James Billington, without admitting or denying his guilt.

Chapter 39 – Auntie Sarah

Mrs. Sarah Hebden, was a 62-year-old insurance premium collector. Who worked for the Royal Liver Friendly Society in Hull, was certainly a woman of some means. She owned her own home and had a regular income of £2. A woman, whose habits were regular, she was careful and orderly.

The premiums she collected amounted to some £5 weekly, she would always visit the office of the insurance company on a Thursday morning of each week taking along her books and paid the money into the cash office.

While at home the books and money was always kept in a brown paper bag on the table in the parlour. She generally had at home as well as the insurance money, £5 to £10 emergency money, which was kept locked in a tea caddy on the bedside table in her bedroom.

A small amount of 'everyday money', consisting of silver and copper was kept in the kitchen drawer.

Fortnightly after paying in the premiums Sarah would either take a train to Leeds, where she would visit her foster daughter – Alice Appleton, or to a village called Elloughton to visit some friends.

She would stay at either location until the Sunday night or early the Monday morning, before returning home and going on her insurance round.

On Thursday 14th November 1901, Sarah had gone to Leeds; her foster daughter gave her a present of a small metal brooch. She boarded the train on Monday morning, wearing a gold watch and gold chain with the brooch in her handbag.

She went to work as usual that week and was heard cleaning her fire grate out at 11pm on the evening of Wednesday 28th November.

The next morning a girl called Jackson called round the Sarah's house at 9am, the house was in darkness with no sign of Sarah.

She went round to a neighbour a Mrs. Bower who also happened to be Sarah's sister, telling her that Sarah was not at home. Mrs. Bower knew her sister was regimental in her habits walked round to Sarah's house. She checked round the outside of the house, heard nothing inside and immediately became suspicious.

Mrs. Bower made her way to the offices of the insurance company to check whether Sarah had paid the premiums in that morning, she was told that Sarah had not arrived at the office as usual.

She returned home and waited for her daughter Francis to come back. She did so at 4.30pm that afternoon, then both women went to Sarah's house to investigate further. They found a kitchen window, which was unlatched, and Francis managed to climb through.

Almost straight away the battered body of Mrs. Hebden was found. The police were called and searched the house.

Behind a box in the bedroom the collecting books and two purses where found. One purse contained £3 12s 2d. The other being empty. The tea caddy normally kept locked and on the bedside table, was found under the bed, broken open and the contents missing. The gold chain was found, but the gold watch and metal brooch had disappeared.

Arthur Richardson, 26, a joiner was the illegitimate son of Mrs. Bower, he knew his aunts habits and that money was kept in the house.

He had married in March 1901, but not long after he had been convicted of robbing another aunt at Brigg. Richardson was sentenced to 6 months imprisonment, which was served at Lincoln jail.

On Wednesday 20th November he had been released from custody, along with his personal money he was given by the prison

167

6s 2d amounting to 9s 2d in total. Richardson travelled to Hull and lodged with a friend in Faith Terrace, Walker Street, by the name of Skelton. He was given another 2s 6d which Richardson's wife had asked Mrs. Skelton to pass onto him.

Mr. Skelton and Richardson left the house on the morning November 25th, Skelton to go to work and Richardson to seek work, Richardson went back to the house at approx. 11.30am saying that he had secured a position in Hull where he would be paid 26s a week.

The next few mornings he left with Mr. Skelton for the walk to Hull, both men parting company along the walk each heading off in separate directions.

On November 28th Richardson parted company with Skelton as had become normal and met a Mr. Fenton at Alexandra dock, Hull. To get to Alexandra Dock he would have had to pass his aunt's house.

Fenton and Richardson stood talking for a few minutes; Richardson kept jingling the loose change in his pocket throughout the conversation. He told Fenton that his aunt had been robbed and murdered, he was living of the land, but now having plenty of money he advised Fenton to try out his winning gambling scheme.

That morning Richardson went to a tailor and purchased an overcoat for £1. 15s, he was also measured for a new suit costing £3 and gave his name as Kennedy, living at a false address.

He returned to the Skelton's home in the evening, Mr. Skelton noticed that his left hand was badly bruised, Richardson passed it off as an accident at work. He took out a gold watch from his pocket, which Mr. Skelton had not seen before and asked if he had a key to wind it up.

Richardson was arrested on the 30th November and taken to the police station for questioning. When searched the police found on him, a gold watch, which was later identified as Mrs. Hebden's.

The metal brooch was found, again it was Mrs. Hebden's and the sum of £1. 15s.

In questioning about the money Richardson said that, "When he was arrested in Scarborough the previous March he had hidden in his sock a £10 note, the money had not been found and this was what he had been spending recently."

With regard to the watch he said, "I had pawned the watch in March and throw away the pawn ticket, but managed to get it back without the stub just the other day."

The police interviewed the tailor who said that when he measured Richardson the clothes he was wearing were wet and soiled.

The police examined these clothes and found blood on his boots, coat, vest, shirt, cuffs and trousers. When this evidence was put to Richardson he replied, "I can explain the blood, but I will reserve the answer for my trial."

Richardson was charged with the murder of Sarah Hebden and appeared at the Assizes at York in March 1902. The presiding judge Mr. Justice Lawrence instructed Mr. Kershaw to act for the defendant; Mr. Milvain and Mr. Cantley conducted the prosecution.

In the opening statement to the jury, Mr. Cantley said, "The question as to whether or not the prisoner is guilty of murder, depended entirely on circumstantial evidence." Many people were called to the witness box to give this evidence.

Richardson took the stand he stated that Mrs. Hebden had given him the watch on November 25th for him to get it repaired.

The blood that was found on his clothes was from a fight, which he had in March before going to Lincoln prison. The brooch he had bought in Grimsby after being released from prison.

The jury found the prisoner guilty of murder; the learned judge asked Richardson if he had anything to say as to why the sentence of death could not be passed on him.

He replied, "All I have to say is that I am innocent, and the punishment I have to receive is an unjust punishment."
The sentence of death was then passed in the usual way.

Richardson aged 26 was taken away to await the execution which was at Hull prison on the 25th March 1902 the hangman being the Billington brothers.

Chapter 40 – Oh Bill!

Hull marine engineer William James Bolton, a married man but living apart from his wife, had been having a relationship with Jane Elizabeth Allen for sometime. He frequently visited her home at No. 10 Andrew Marvin Terrace, Hull often staying the night.

On the night of October 17th Bolton arrived at her door about 11pm, Jane refused to let him in, telling him that he'd better not come round again as the neighbours have been complaining. She went on to say that his wife had come around earlier and had caused a scene in the street. She didn't want anymore trouble so it would be best to stop things.

The couple talked on the door step for ages and eventually according Jane's lodger, Mrs. Butterick, who was a widow and had lived in the house for a couple of months, Jane allowed Bolton in to the house and they went upstairs together at about 12.30 am,

Jane asked Mrs. Butterick to give her an early morning call around 6.50am and then closed the bedroom door. Mrs Butterick slept on the sofa which she had always done, but was awoken at 6.30 am by Jane screaming, "Oh Bill, don't".

This was heard 3 times so Mrs. Butterick went upstairs to the bedroom that the couple was occupying. Walking into the room she saw Jane lying on the bed, near the wall bleeding. Bolton was laid next to Jane holding a knife, his throat was bleeding and he was groaning.

The knife was similar to the one that Bolton always used to cut his tobacco. Mrs. Butterick dragged Jane over Bolton, allowing her to fall onto the floor, where she laid helpless and unconscious. Knowing that there was nothing that she could do herself to help Jane, Mrs. Butterick ran out of the house to fetch the police.

She returned half an hour later with two police constables, P.C. Barton and P.C. Shaw. As they walked through the front door Bolton was walking down the stairs, blood coming from his neck wound that was obvious that it had been self-inflicted but was not

The crimes behind the hangings

life threatening. P.C. Burton asked him what he had done, Bolton replied. "I don't know". They went to the bedroom and found Jane dead on the floor. The knife was under the bed, the blade was open and there was blood on the blade and handle.

Bolton was taken to the Infirmary for treatment; it was there where he said to P.C. Shaw, "I don't know what made me do it." Bolton was treated for his wounds and was released in the custody of the police who charged him on the 20th October with murder.

He made no comment to the charge at the time, but as P.C. Shaw was putting him back in the cell he is alleged to have said, "The inspector need not have said anything to me, all I have to say is that I am guilty."

The prisoner was brought before the Assizes at York in front of Mr. Justice Channell, Mr. H.T. Kemp and Mr. Brent Grotian prosecuted on behalf of the treasury. Mr. Mortimer represented the prisoner.

Dr. Lamb gave evidence that Jane Allen had received three fatal wounds, these could not and would not have been self inflicted.

The prisoner then gave his evidence, "I have no knowledge of having stabbed the woman, I was awaken by the Jane crying out 'Oh Bill, are you mad, what are you doing?' Seeing what I had done I attempted to cut my own throat but was stopped by Jane, I asked Mrs. Butterick to go quickly and fetch someone to help. While she was gone, Jane sat up on the floor and said to me that I had attacked her in my sleep, she tried but could not get any sense out of me."

On being asked about the knife he replied, "After we had gone upstairs I had cut some tobacco, and had left the knife open, on a box near the head of the bed."

Mr. Mortimer addressed the jury on behalf of Bolton said, "If Mr. Bolton attacked the woman in his sleep he could not be convicted of anything, but if he was in a semi-conscious condition at the time he would not be guilty of anything more than manslaughter."

He made further comments about the affectionate relationship that had existed between the prisoner and the deceased.

Mr. Justice Channell in summing up to the jury said that, "If the stabs were consciously inflicted he did not think that the crime committed could be less than murder."

With regards to the evidence he went on to say, "The evidence which Mr. Bolton has given is in direct contradiction to that of the evidence given by Dr. Lamb and Mrs. Butterrick."

In conclusion he said, "In my opinion, the jury could not find the prisoner guilty of manslaughter, it is a case of murder."

The jury did not leave the court to consider their verdict, almost immediately they returned the verdict of guilty.

The judge then sentenced William James Bolton to death and ordered for him to be taken away. He was taken to Hull prison where he was executed on the 23rd December 1902 by the Billington brothers.

Chapter 41 – Farm Hands

Ann Marshall aged 16 and 19 year old Charles Ashton, were both in the employment of Mr. George Brewster at his farm at Scampton Grange, Malton. The employment included bed and board therefore they both lived on the farm. Ann was a religious girl and would always go to church on a Sunday evening the church she regularly attended was at Rillington, a small village near by, this required a walk of about 3 miles, which Ann did week after week.

On Sunday 20th September 1903 Ann left the farm as usual for the walk to Rillington Church, she was expected to return to the farm that evening at around 9pm but she failed to arrive. At 9.30pm two gunshots and a scream some distance from the farm was to be heard, George Brewster went outside, couldn't see anything, nothing more was heard so he went back into the farmhouse.

Charles Ashton had also gone for a walk on that evening he returned back to the farmhouse at 10.30pm, later than what George normally allowed. George asked Ashton if he had heard the gunshots, which he said that he did but did not see anything and could not tell exactly where the shots had come from.

The following morning Ann still had not returned to the farm, George Brewster was getting more anxious as to where Ann was, and He asked Ashton whether he had seen her. Ashton replied that he had seen her last evening at the gate to the cricket field, but had not seen her since. No sightings or signs of Ann's whereabouts were made throughout the rest of the day.

The following day, Tuesday, Ashton was carting corn from a field, he went up to the other workers and said, "Here is Annie's hat, I have found it in a wheat field." He carried the wet hat to the farm, the police were called, and Ashton waited along with Mr. Brewster for the police constable to arrive.

When police constable Broughton got at the farm, Ashton described the place where he had found the hat, the constable asked him to take him there and show him exactly where he had come across it. The three men went to the wheat field; there was nowhere in the field that fitted the description of where Ashton had supposedly found the wet hat, the ground being totally dry.

Ashton said to both men, "My opinion is that someone has killed her and carried her to the Black-bridge and thrown her into the river, on Sunday night I saw three poachers and heard two shots fired, something screamed like a hare but it might have been a child."

The three men then walked to a Barley field, which Ashton had said he thought that the gunshots had come from. On reaching the field Ashton said, "No I don't think that she will be here, she will be down by the river." They walked half a mile or so down to the river, where the prisoner straight away pointed out something laid in the river at the side of the bank.

The police constable immediately investigated what this was and found the dead body of Ann Marshall. The body was placed in a cart and taken to the farm, on examination, two bullets were found in the girl's cheek. The bone at the base of the skull was found to be fractured, along with signs that showed that the girl had suffered from considerable violence before she died.

Constable Broughton was very suspicious at the story that Ashton had given him regarding finding the hat, and even more concern about how he had acted in the field prior to finding the dead girl, he arrested Ashton on suspicion of committing murder. Ashton immediately said that he knew nothing of the murder and repeated this statement at the police station. He was searched and his property recorded then placed a prisoner's property locker. Along with other items there was a key and a purse.

The police searched Ashton's room at the farm, where they found a locked box, the police sergeant remembering that Ashton had a key taken from him at the police station when he was searched, took the box down to the station. The key was taken out of Ashton's property it opened the box. Inside they found clothes that were covered in blood, in the pocket of a coat, was a revolver. Ashton was then charged with the murder of Ann Marshall.

Ashton later that evening admitted the murder and wrote and signed a statement to that effect.

The Assizes at York on the 1st December 1903 before Mr. Justice Grantham was where Ashton stood trial. Mr. T. Milvain and Mr. F. Brent Grotrian prosecuted the case, and Mr. R.H. Vernon Wragge defended the prisoner.

The written statement which Aston had wrote confessing to the crime which was read out in court, was the basis of the prosecution case. Along with the circumstantial evidence, that he had blood on his clothes and a revolver, which was the same calibre as the bullets, found in the body of Ann.

Mr. Wragge for the prisoner insisted that there was no motive for the horrendous crime. The prisoner had previously been of good character and he had been on good terms with Ann. He admitted that Ashton had a temper and everything pointed to there being a struggle where upon Ashton had used the revolver in the heat of the moment.

The learned judge in his summing up to the jury said that, "The absence of a motive is not an excuse for the crime."

The jury retired and a short while later returned to the court and found the prisoner guilty of murder with a strong recommendation of mercy on account of the prisoners age.

His lordship passed the sentence of death and the prisoner was taken to Hull prison to wait his execution, which was later set for the morning of the 22nd December 1903, by the two brothers from the family of executioners William and John Billington.

Chapter 42 - Good Morning John

Emily, a little small, round faced woman standing at only 4ft 10" tall and aged 42 was the mother of 11 children. She was married to William Swann a glass blower. They both lived a respectable life in the suburbs of Barnsley, in a little village called Wombwell. John Gallagher a miner aged 30, was their lodger for a while living at the same address, he became intimate with Emily, but William Swann found out about this affair and asked him to leave.

It was common knowledge to the neighbours that William often beat his wife, the beatings became more severe after he had found out about the affair between the couple.

Gallagher having moved out of the Swann's house had moved in with Mrs. Ward a neighbour who lived opposite the Swann's. Emily would visit Mrs. Ward on a regular basis, this always resulted in Emily and William arguing and more often than not, a couple of fists been thrown by William in Emily's direction. Gallagher decided if he moved out of the area, things would settle down between the couple, so he decided that he would move on to Bradford.

On the 6th June, Gallagher was in the kitchen of his lodgings when Emily came to the house, they sat down and had a couple of drinks together. Emily had to pop across the road, back to her own house for a minute leaving Gallagher and Mrs. Ward drinking in the parlour.

She returned a few minutes later, her head covered with a shawl, she sat down and said, "Look what our Bill has done." She removed the shawl and showed her friend the two black eyes and the bruising to her face. Seeing the state of Emily's face, Gallagher immediately became riled and said, "I will give him something for himself for that,"

He left the house and went straight over to the Swann's house. On the way across the street Gallagher was heard by another neighbour to say, "I will coffin him before the morning!"

Gallagher rushed in to the Swann's house, closely followed by Emily, the sound of violent altercation was to be heard for what was described as 10 minutes. Gallagher then left the house and walked back to the neighbours hand in hand with Emily.

At the house he was to say, "I've busted four of his ribs and I'll bust four more." He seemed to calm down for a few minutes and then announced, "I'll finish him before I go to Bradford." He went into another rage, setting off back towards the Swann's residence he shouted, "I'll murder the pig before morning, if he can't kick a man, he shouldn't kick a woman,"

Gallagher went straight in to the Swann's house, closely followed by Emily. Another fight started and Emily was heard to say, "Go on Johnny give it to him."

Five minutes later Gallagher emerged from the house and walked over to Mrs. Wards leaving Emily at her own home. Shortly afterwards, Emily walked over to Mrs. Ward's and asked her to come over as her husband was dead.

The police was called for, they went to Swann's house, found William dead, the house being smashed to pieces in what was immediately apparent had been a most violent attack.

Emily was arrested but Gallagher had disappeared. He had slipped out of the back door and had gone on the run, living rough until eventually turning up at a relatives house in Middlesbrough where he was arrested 2 months later on the 4th August.

Gallagher and Swann were both charged with the murder of William Swann and appeared together at the Leeds Assizes in October 1903 in front of Mr. Justice Darling. Mr. Tindal-Atkinson and Mr. W.J. Waugh conducted the prosecution. Mr. Mitchell-Innes represented Gallagher and Mr. Harold Newell appeared for Swann.

The case was and open and shut case according to the prosecution, the prisoners had been in a immoral relationship, the husband had found out, raised his hand to his wife, and in retribution the boyfriend while his sweetheart urged him on, had made the husband pay, with his life.

The defence insisted that neither prisoner wanted the victim dead. Emily had not taken part in the fight, nor had she raised a hand to her husband, therefore she should be released without charge. As for Gallagher, he had no intention of killing Mr. Swann, he had merely been involved in a fight with the deceased that had resulted in a tragic death, and a verdict of manslaughter should be reached.

His lordship on summing up the evidence to the jury said. "Gallagher's remark of; I'll finish him before I go to Bradford, which was allegedly made between the two fights, showed intent. As for the woman, one does not commit murder only with one's hands, if one person instigates another to commit murder and the other person does it, the instigator is also guilty of murder."

The jury taking only an hour to deliberate returned to the court and hardly surprising they found both the prisoners guilty of murder. The judge before passing sentence of death asked both the prisoners if they had anything to say. Emily stood up and said, "I am innocent, I am not afraid of immediate death because I am innocent and I will go to God."

Emily looked undisturbed when she was led from the dock; she waved and blew a kiss to someone in the crowd. They were both taken to the cells below the court to wait for transport to take them to separate condemned cells at Armley jail to await the executioner.

Meanwhile back in the courtroom, the judge before discharging the jury, said that. "He was aware of evidence that was withheld from the courtroom, this evidence," he said, "In my opinion, proved that Swann had taken part in the murder of her husband."

He read a statement to the jury, "When Gallagher was taken into custody, he made a statement to the police that Emily hit William and beat him with a poker. This statement was not direct evidence but from the position of where the poker had subsequently been found, it would appear to be true. As the statement was hearsay and would jeopardise Swann's defence, it had been decided not to allow this evidence".

The prosecution was happy, they had managed to secure a conviction without the vital piece of evidence, withholding that evidence was deemed to be an example of the fairness of the British judicial system.

Both prisoners lodged an appeal against their sentences; Gallagher had not expected to be reprieved and resigned himself to the fact that he would soon die.

Emily though, thought that she would be. When she was informed by the Governor of that her reprieve had been turned down, she became distressed and collapsed. She was constantly worried that she had brought great disgrace on her children and family, her children worked endlessly to help her, raising a petition and even writing to the King begging for clemency, this was as usual ignored.

The two condemned prisoners were always kept apart in the jail, if one was out of their cell the other one would be locked up in their own cell. The only time that they set eyes on each other before the execution was at the Christmas morning church service, in the prison chapel. They were kept well apart by the warders watching them both 24 hours away, and were not allowed even to make eye contact.

It was decided that the two would be hanged together and on the morning of the 29th December, John Billington assisted by John Ellis, took Gallagher to the execution room, pinioned him and placed the white hood over his head. They put the noose round his neck and adjusted it; Gallagher then stood waiting for the trap to be released.

Emily in the meantime was finding it extremely difficult to be composed, Billington and Ellis went to her cell to collect her, finding her laid on the floor in a pitiful state, her warders encouraging her to stand and be brave. Ellis administrated a large dose of Brandy to her, which seemed have the desired effect and she was taken to the execution room. She could see that Gallagher was standing on the trap door and she was placed directly behind him.

Gallagher was waiting patiently unaware what the delay was when he heard, "Good morning John." it was Swann, he found it hard to speak but managed in a quite voice to reply, "Good morning love."

The noose was placed around Swann's neck and she cried out, "Goodbye, God bless you." The trap was released and both the prisoners were hanged.

Emily Swann was the only female to be executed in the history of Armley jail, and the first of only 3 female executions in which John Ellis was involved in.

The other two female hangings were Edith Thompson, who's case was similar to Swann's (The killing of her husband by her boyfriend) and the hanging of Susan Newell, who at the gallows refused to wear the white hood. Ellis disliked executing females that he refused to take part in anymore.

Chapter 43 – The Poachers

44 year old Arthur Jefferies and his friend since childhood, Samuel Baker, met the night of November 12th for a drink at a local inn near Rotherham. Both men were poachers and Samuel informed Jefferies that he had been poaching with the group of three friends that were with him, without Jefferies knowledge. Jefferies was livid about not being invited and an argument ensued between the two men.

Baker and his three friends left the pub at around 11pm that evening for the short stroll home, Jefferies ran passed them and down an alley way which led to his house. When the group approached the entrance to the alley a couple of minutes later, they noticed that Jefferies was stood there with his wife.

According to evidence given by one of the group of me a Mr. Morris, Jefferies was holding a long thin instrument of some kind.

Samuel Baker said, "Goodnight mate." directed at Jefferies. Jefferies replied using abusive language and struck Baker, who retaliated by grabbing Jefferies by the collar and pushing him into the alley. Sounds of a struggle were heard and a couple of seconds later Baker came out of the alley and almost instantly fell dead.

The coroner said that Baker had an 8" deep wound to his side, which had severed his Aorta, a long sharp instrument had caused this wound.

Mr. T. R. D. Wright for the prosecution told the jury that Jefferies had a history of violence and had said on occasions, while under the influence of drink, "That he would do for one of them before long."

Jefferies pleaded not guilty to the charge of murder and his defence led by Mr. Coutts-Trotter asked the jury to accept a plea of guilty to the lesser charge of manslaughter.

He stated that the killing was not premeditated, both men had been life long friends. No weapon had been found, nobody had witnessed the fatal blow and it most possibly had been struck in the course of a fight in the alley. In all the years of the two men being friends, Jefferies had never shown any violence towards Mr. Baker.

Mr. Justice Grantham, the judge presiding at Leeds Assizes, who as a country squire, often had his own land used by poachers.

He was notoriously well known for his hatred of poachers and agreed with the prosecution in his summing up of the case. He said, "If Arthur Jefferies killed Samuel Baker, whether it be in the course of a struggle or premeditated, then the only possible verdict that could be reached was guilty of murder".

The jury reached their verdict of guilty of murder in the double quick time, 30 minutes in all. They strongly recommended mercy to the judge, but to no avail.

Mr. Justice Grantham donned his black cap, sentenced Arthur Jefferies to death by hanging and ordered him to be taken down.

John Billington and Henry Pierrepoint hanged Jefferies on the 28th December 1904 at Armley gaol.

Chapter 44 – Middlesbrough Murder

Mary Lynas a harmless 12 year old girl lived at 17 Bennison Street, Guisborough. On the night of the 27th December 1903 she left the friends she had been to church with, and carried on the short walk back to her house alone. At around 8pm when she failed to appear home, her mother started to get anxious so the police were called and a search was mounted for the girl.

The police searched the local woods and fields, shortly afterwards her body was found near to the Guisborough work house by Sergeant Lambert, her hands and legs where tied with a clothes line, she had been placed in a kneeling position and her throat was cut from ear to ear.

A trial of blood led from where Mary was found and it was eventually traced to 9 Bennison Street. The home of a Mr. Clarkson and family, there was blood on the back door step, and in the coal shed outside they found blood stained papers and Mary's hat was found.

Mr. Clarkson said that his nineteen year old son had come home at 9.30pm, he wasn't excited, and he seemed quite composed at the time. He had shortly afterwards gone upstairs to bed. The police officers went up to the bedroom and arrested James Clarkson.

The house was then searched from top to bottom, Clarkson's clothes were stained with blood and in the kitchen cupboard they came across a razor which had traces of blood on it. This later was proved to be the blood of Mary.

Clarkson seem totally unconcerned from the outset, he pleaded not guilty throughout the preliminary hearings and was eventually sent for trial at the York Assizes in front of Mr. Justice Lawrence.

The prosecution team was Mr. T.V. Malvain and Mr. H.B Grotain; Mr. Shortt represented the defendant.

Medical evidence was called regarding the cause of death, even though the girl's throat had been cut there were no other injuries to her. She had a deep gash severing her jugular vein, the gash running from ear to hear.

Doctor Bevan the medical Superintendent of Wakefield Asylum was called to give evidence on the prisoner's mental health, he had an hour and half consultation with the prisoner and stated that the prisoner was suffering from grave moral perversion and was unconcerned about the crime he was charged with. He was also of unsound mind, he knows what is happening at this time, but doesn't understand the seriousness of what is happening.

Police superintendent Holmes said, "The night the prisoner was arrested we had call for concern over his behaviour he was crying out why did I do it what made me do it."

The prisoners shouted from the witness box, "No way did I say anything like that!"

Mr. Shortt for the prisoner in his summing up said that, "At no point in the evidence that the prosecution have produced, is there any proof that the prisoner did commit the murder. If he did commit the murder, did they prove that the prisoner was sane at the time of the murder? The point was." He continued, "An horrific murder was committed, Mr. Clarkson has no recollection of committing the murder, and it was proved that the doctor called to give evidence said the prisoner mind was unstable and he had doubts about his sanity."

The jury retired and shortly afterwards returned the verdict of murder. Clarkson aged 19 was taken away and hung on the 29th March 1904 at Armley gaol by William Billington.

Chapter 45 – Voices In My Head

John Thomas Kay aged 52, a dark bearded, medium sized man lived with his girlfriend in Sheffield Road, Rotherham. The couple had lived together for only 3 months. Jane has split with her husband before meeting Kay. The relationship was not a happy one, they both drunk to excess and were very quarrelsome with each other.

Easter Monday 1904, the couple had been drinking, an argument started, which was common between the couple. Kay grabbed Jane and threw her out on to the street. Telling her that she was not coming in anymore, he'd had enough.

A neighbour, Mrs. Robinson pleaded with Kay to allow Jane back in. He eventually relented but said to Mrs. Robinson, "If I do I will finish her tonight with a knife."

Things seemed to settle down at the Kay residence for a while, but on Saturday 7th May another argument started, Jane packed some clothes and left, vowing never to return. She did however come back on the Monday 9th May. She was seen going into the house at 10.30pm, never to be seen alive again.

Kay left his house on the Tuesday 10th May 1904 at 5.30am. He walked round the streets of Rotherham and eventually came across a policeman. He asked the copper for directions to the police station. The policeman asked him what he wanted the station for; Kay just shrugged of the question saying he would explain when he got there.

A couple of minutes later Kay said. "I might as well tell you, its murder I think. It's a woman I live with. Not the wife! I did it with a hatchet, I hit her three or four times, I don't know how many, but she is dead."

Kay was taken to the police station; other constables went to the house in Sheffield Road. Jane was still alive; but she was unconscious, with four gaping wounds to her head. A doctor was called for, but Jane died before he had time to treat her.

Kay was charged with murder and after the preliminary hearings he was sent for trial at the Assizes in Leeds in front of Mr. Justice Channell. Mr. Harold Thomas and Mr. Ball appeared for the prosecution and Mr. Mitchell-Innes represented Kay.

The prosecution called for medical evidence, which showed that Jane's skull had been smashed in four places. Each blow would have rendered her unconscious and eventually killed her.

Mrs. Robinson gave evidence regarding the couples arguments, their drinking habits and Kay's constant jealousy because of Jane's friendship with a lodger.

The policeman gave evidence as to the conversation that he had with Kay on the morning of the 10th May.

The defence did not dispute the facts of the case. The only defence was the alleged condition of the prisoner's mind that fateful morning.

Kay took the stand and gave evidence that around April 5th he had caught Jane with one of the lodgers. It affected him so much that he had stopped working and started drinking. On May 7th he had tried twice to hang himself with a picture cord. This didn't work as the cord kept snapping.

He went to bed on the 9th May at around 11pm. He didn't know how long that he had slept, but he woke hearing voices telling him to kill her. He went downstairs got the hatchet and hit her while she slept. "I don't remember how many times I hit her, but as I was doing it a great weight was lifted from my mind. When I saw what I had done, I ran down the stairs and found a policeman."

"Before you heard the voices, had you ever thought about killing her?" Asked Mr. Mitchell-Innes.

"Certainly not!" Replied Kay, "I had arranged the removal of my furniture and I was going to move to Hull out of the way."

The defence called Dr. Clarke, Medical Officer of Wakefield prison he said. "If a man had been persistently drinking and was at the same under influence of a sentiment of jealousy these things would increase his liability to an attack of impulsive insanity. A previous history of suicide would show that the man had a tendency to this impulsive action. An impression on the part of the prisoner that voices were urging him to commit the deed would point to mental derangement. The subsequent calmness of the prisoner and clearness of memory were quite consistent with an attack of impulsive insanity."

Dr. Clarke concluded by saying. "On the night of the murder he woke suddenly and a strange feeling came over him. He heard a voice whisper do it, kill her. Assuming these statements were correct the man would have no knowledge of right or wrong. Beyond what the prisoner has told me I have not observed any evidence of insanity."

The judge said, "So basically, what you are saying is that, anyone can murder and then say that they had heard voices in their head telling them to do it." He then summed up the case to the jury.

The jury retired and returned only 25 minutes later with the verdict of guilty of murder.

The judge addressed Kay, sentenced him to death in the usual way and then said, "Do not allow any hope that you may have mercy from any man to interfere with your efforts to seek mercy of God, of which you stand so surely in need."

Kay was taken to Armley jail and was executed on the 16th August 1904 by William Billington.

Chapter 46 – York Murder

John Dalby, a frail 78 year old man, lived alone at Alba Terrace, York. His daughter had married and moved out of the area. She lived at Armley Road, Leeds, and a very short walk from Armley jail. In fact she would see the prison everyday, when she was going about her daily chores. It was hard to miss being a big imposing building that was built on a hill at the side of Armley Road, it could be seen from miles away in every direction. Even today it's one of the first buildings which can be seen when approaching Leeds from the west or south.

Undoubtedly she would never have imagined on the morning of the 29th July when she woke up, that her father would be brutally murdered, or that the murderer would be housed in the jail and would be executed in the very place which she saw everyday of her life.

The executed prisoners were buried on the North side of the prison. All that stood between the North side of the jail and Armley Road was the prison wall, how could anyone face life knowing that behind those walls would soon be the unmarked grave of the man who had murdered her frail father in the most brutal of murders. The grave would contain the executed body of a man called Edmund Hall, the man she had married, loved and who had been welcomed warmly into her family.

Former soldier, 49 year old Hall had served in the army in India between 1874 –1879 and again 1880-1882, he had been discharged in 1879 suffering from melancholia due to sunstroke, but had re-enlisted in 1880 for another 2 years serving in India.

Since his last discharge he had worked in Woolwich, London at an engineering works, then he moved to Leeds, where he settled at Armley Road. He had suffered a bad injury while working in a lift; this also brought on depression and mood changes.

On the afternoon of the 29th July, Hall boarded a train to York. He turned up at this father in laws home in the early evening, John Dalby opened the door and Hall went inside.

Shortly afterwards the neighbours heard a scuffle, followed by some groans, so two men Mr. Jagger and Mr. Liddell ran round to the back door to investigate. The back door opened and Dalby staggered out, holding his throat. Mr. Jagger shouted for someone to get a doctor.

Hall rushed out of the house saying, "I'll go and get one." He then jumped over the brick wall and disappeared into the distance.

John Dalby was eventually taken to the hospital where his throat was treated along with various other minor wounds. John died in the early hours of the morning, without speaking a word of what had happened.

Meanwhile, the police had a description of Edmund Hall and were searching for him. They went to the train station, they couldn't believe their luck, Hall was sat on the Leeds bound train waiting for it to depart. He was smoking a cigar and appeared quite calm. He was arrested and taken in for questioning.

The house at Alma Terrace was searched, furniture and ornaments were smashed, on the floor in the room they found a bar from a watch chain, which was connected to a spade guinea, the watch and chain was missing. The neighbours identified the property of being Mr. Dalby's. The prisoner when he was arrested was found to be wearing the missing watch and chain.

Edmund Hall was charged with the murder and remanded in custody, the court case was held at York in front of Mr. Justice Darling. Mr. Wilberforce and Mr. Grotian prosecuted the case; Mr. Mortimer defended the prisoner.

The evidence was not contested; Hall admitted the murder, but pleaded insanity.

The defence called Dr. Clark the medical officer of Wakefield prison to give evidence to the prisoner's state of mind.

He said, "In my opinion with regard to the prisoners history, it was possible that a very small cause would drive him into a violent insanity and his physical condition at the time was compatible with such an hypothesis."

Mr. Mortimer addressing the jury said. "The prisoner was on very good terms with his father in law, something must have been said for him to react the way that he did, then commit the murder. This was not the action of a sane man, therefore you the jury have no alternative than to find the prisoner not guilty."

The jury did nothing of the kind, he was found guilty of wilful murder and sentenced to death.

John Billington executed him on the 20th December 1904 and he was buried on the North side of the jail, just yards away from his home.

Chapter 47 – The Plasterer

Thomas Tattersall aged 31, his wife of 12 years and 4 children lived in Wakefield; Thomas was a plasterer, earning relatively good money. Home life was not a happy one for the Tattersall's. Thomas had once tried to take his own life; he regularly suffered from influenza and had turned to spending most of his evenings drinking.

The arguments between the couple continued throughout early 1905, these seemed to be getting more and more violent, one occasion he grabbed her round the throat and threatened to do her. An another occasion after he had been drinking he attempted to strangle her, regaining his composure before he killed her.

The police were informed about the violent outbursts at the home. They put on extra patrols past the house so they could listen and more sure things were quiet. Rebecca asked her brother on more than one occasion if he would protect her, but that didn't seem to work.

Three weeks before the murder of Rebecca, the arguments got more frequent, she begged her brother to help, which he agreed to do. He had a word with Tattersall, and things seemed to quieten down for the time being.

July 3rd 1905, in the early hours of the morning there was a gurgling sound heard by Tattersall's daughter, it was coming from her parents bedroom, she climbed the stairs to go and investigate, when she met her father coming down towards her. He said, "I you scream I will murder you."

The little girl managed to raise the alarm, the police were called, when they entered the bedroom, Rebecca was laid on the bed, her head been badly beaten and her throat was cut. They found a bloodstained axe in the room along with a razor that had been used to slit her throat.

Tattesall was arrested for the wilful murder of his wife and made a confession saying that he had attacked Rebecca with a hatchet then cut her throat, but he did not know what he was doing.

When he was searched at the police station, they found a small knife carefully concealed within his clothing, this could quite possibly have been used to do himself harm while waiting for his trial.

Tattersall was placed in custody and appeared at the NorthEastern Assizes held at Leeds on the 30th July 1905. Mr. Longstaffe and Mr. Ball conducted the prosecution. Mr. Mellor represented Tattersall.

The defence did not dispute any of the facts of the murder, what they did say was. "The prisoner regularly suffered from influenza and had attempted suicide, combined with the prisoners drinking habits it was sufficient to show that he wasn't responsible for his actions at the time of the murder."

Mr. Justice Jelf in his summing up to the jury said, "Medical evidence was shown to the effect that there was nothing to indicate actual insanity."

The jury agreed with the judge and found the prisoner guilty of murder; the death sentence was passed in the usual way.

Tattersall was taken away to Armley jail to await the execution which was set for 16 days after the trial.

Most prisoners at this point, would have any idea what to expect, they wouldn't know the layout of the condemned cell or the hanging cell, but Tattersall knew exactly what to expect. He had just finished work on the execution chamber at Wakefield jail, ready for its first execution in 1906.

14th August 1905, the day before the execution, the hangman and his assistant arrived as normal to the prison. In this particular execution John Billington was the hangman and his assistant

William Warbrick who had been called back on to the list due to shortages of assistants.

The gallows were being prepared ready for the execution the next day; Billington took a step backwards and fell through the open trap door.

He was well enough to carry on with the execution the following day, but this would be his last one, he died a few weeks later at this home in Chorley, Lancashire. The case of death was stated as Dropsy, but many believe it was due to internal injuries suffered from falling through the trap door.

Chapter 48 – 49 Stabs

George and Martha Smith, had 2 children, Smith found it difficult to find work as a bricklayers labourer due to his age. Martha had no alternative than to go and get work herself, and send money back to look after Smith and the children. She went into domestic service, where she received full board and lodgings, this meant her small wage, which was enough to look after the rest of the family.

Martha started work for a gentleman called Mr. Skelton; he was a prawn-broker and lived in a rather nice house near Leeds. Martha worked for him for a while, but Smith didn't like the man and ordered his wife to stop working there. He would do for her if she refused. Martha didn't have much choice so she left Mr. Skelton's employment and went to stay at her parent's home in Wakefield.

Martha heard about a job working for a gentleman called Mr. Glendenning, in Ilkley, she applied for the job and was successful. Smith was living at a lodging house at Park Lane, Leeds owned by a Mrs. Storey.

The new job suited Martha, she was alone most of the day, Mr. Glendenning being away a lot of the time, and his daughter Catherine was always of shopping and socialising. This suited Martha well, she got on with her job without being constantly disrupted.

On the morning of the 12th September 1905, Martha had been busy doing the washing; it was a fine day so she hung it out on the washing line in the garden. Catherine Glendenning had gone of to Leeds shopping with friends.

Meanwhile Smith was getting ready to leave the lodging house, when Mrs. Storey stopped him and asked whether he had the rent money.

Smith said. "I am waiting for Martha to send the money to me, it will be here in a couple of days. I am going to Halifax for an interview for a job."

The crimes behind the hangings

Catherine returned to the house from shopping, the back door was locked from the inside, she had to go round to the front door and gain access that way.

She called out for Martha, but got no reply. She walked into the kitchen, the walls and floor were covered in blood, Martha was laid dead on the floor, her clothes were covered in blood from the numerous cuts to her body, there was a large cut to her throat.

The police and a doctor were called, Martha was pronounced dead at 7.20pm. The police searched the house and grounds for clues, the net door neighbour told them that she saw Mrs. Smith at 2.30pm, attending to the washing on the line, she also said that Mrs. Smith was in the house when she left at 4pm.

Nothing seemed to be missing, so burglary was ruled out, this was a murder case and nothing less. The obvious place to start was at the home of the husband. They located the address in the belongings of Martha and sent a constable to Leeds to interview him.

At Park Lane, Leeds, Mrs. Storey told the police that she had not seen Smith since he left that morning, on his way for an interview in Halifax. She hid however give them a full description of him and also the clothes he was wearing. She assured them that should Smith return she would immediately contact them.

The description was circulated to the local police forces and was also given to the police who were conducting house to house searches in Ilkley and surrounding areas.

A girl recognised the description as the man who she had spoke to the previous afternoon in Burley in Wharfedale. (Burley is on the main route between Leeds and Ilkley). This man had asked for directions to a house in Ilkley at around 2.30pm in the afternoon.

It was certain now that the man who had murdered Martha was her husband, the police were searching for him everywhere he might have a connection. Two days after the murder, at 5.30am a police constable was patrolling the streets in the city of Wakefield, a man walked passed him and said, "Good morning." Immediately recognising him as George Smith, he called upon the assistance of another constable and walked up to Smith saying, "You know what we want you for!"

Smith replied, "That's a good cop." He was arrested and taken to Otley police station for questioning. His clothes contained small particles of blood, and also he was wearing a hanky chief around his neck. This was later confirmed as the property of Mr. Glendenning and had been taken from the washing line, just before or just after the murder.

Smith was charged with the murder of his wife and appeared at the Leeds Assizes on the 7th December 1905. Justice Jelf presided over the case. Mr. Harold Thomas and Mr. R.A. Sheppard prosecuted and Mr. Chapman defended the accused.

The prosecution case was that Smith had premeditatedly murdered his wife, he had called at the home of her employer after 2.30pm that afternoon, walked in through the kitchen door and proceeded in attacking his wife with such ferocity that he stabbed her 50 times, and then slit her throat. He stole whatever money Martha had, then made his escape to Wakefield, hoping that no one would think that he was the murderer. On the way, he had thrown away the murder weapon that still has not been found.

Mr. Thomas called medical evidence as to the cause of death. "There was a large wound to the left of the neck, it ran down the edge of the jugular vein and parallel to the jaw line. It was 3 inches long and 2½ inches deep. Her external and internal carotid artery was severed and the Larynx was cut in half. There were also 49 further lacerations to the body, the time of death was estimated to be between 4.30 and 5.30 the afternoon of the 12 September. The wound would have been caused by a sharp butchers knife." Said the doctor.

Mr. Thomas picked up a knife and said, "Would a knife similar to this have caused the wounds?"

The doctor replied, "Yes, I would say so."

Mrs. Storey was called to the stand by the prosecution. She explained what had happened the morning that Smith had left her house and then said, "Soon afterwards I noticed that a pork knife was missing from the kitchen, I had used it the previous night and had left it on the draining board to dry."

Mr. Thomas showed her the knife that he had shown the doctor. Mrs. Storey identified the knife as being identical to the knife that was missing from her kitchen.

Mr. Skelton took the stand and said, "One day while Mrs. Smith was working for me, I found her hiding in the pantry, it was obvious that she had been beaten about the face, she was covered in cuts and bruises. I later saw her husband in the garden, attempting to grab the attention of Martha, I went out and told him not to come here again."

Another servant from Mr. Shelton's household said, "I once saw Smith rush as his wife and shout that he would swing for her."

The defence put Smith on the stand to give evidence.

He said, "I am a bricklayer by trade, I have been married for 11 years and have 2 children. I had an affectionate wife and I was very fond of her. I did not take the knife from the lodging house; I went to talk to the wife. I walked into the house and she tried to keep me away from her, she told me that she had someone else, she didn't want me any more. She shoved me away from her, I had a penknife and I just went for her in a moment of madness. She hit me with a wooden board, and then tried to grab the penknife, cutting me on the hand"

Mr. Chapman, "It all happened in the passion of the moment?"

"Yes" said Smith, "I had the knife and I stabbed her"

Mr. Chapman, "Then what happened Mr. Smith?"

"My wife fell to the ground, I waited with her until she died. I kissed her and she kissed me, than it was all over."

Mr. Thomas cross-examined Smith. "Why did you slit her throat, with a 3 Inch wound?"

"I didn't do it!"

His lordship, "What Smith? You didn't stab your wife and kill her?"

"Yes I did it, but I don't remember a wound like that to her neck." Replied Smith. "It was only about 1½ inch."

"Well we won't argue over an inch or 2." Mr. Thomas said. "Especially when we have 49 other wounds to discuss."

"I just kept stabbing and stabbing at her," continued Smith.

His lordship said, "Was she trying to defend herself."

"Yes."

"How?" he asked.

"With her hands." Said Smith.

His lordship clearly appalled at what he was hearing said, "You mean to say that you stabbed your wife 49 times, and she tried to defend herself with only her hands? No weapon just her bare hands! How dare she!"

"Well she started it, she ran for me and hit me with a square board." Replied Smith.

The judge summed up the case to the jury they retired at 3.40pm to consider their verdict. They returned to the court at 3.53 and found the prisoner guilty of murder.

The judge said, "It is one of the most brutal murders that it has been my lot to try, or even hear of. If anything would be adding to the wickedness of the thing, it was the attempt that you have tried to justify the murder by alleging that your wife was unfaithful. Your wife was a good and kind wife; she worked hard and sent you money to live off. I am saddened that you have acted the way you have." He then passed the sentence in the usual way and then said. "Take him down now!"

Henry Pierrepoint executed 50 year old George Smith on the 28th December 1905 at Armley jail.

Chapter 49 – Wakefield's 1st

39 year old Harry Walters a miner, lived with his girl friend Sarah Ann McConnell aged 42 at 13 Court, Allen Street, Sheffield. Sarah Ann was a married woman, but she lived apart from her husband.

On the 23rd December 1905 sounds of a quarrel were to be heard by the neighbours coming from the house. A little later at around 4.30 Sarah was seen getting water from the outhouse and then Mrs. Revel a fish hawker called for payment for the fish she supplied early in the week. Sarah told her that she didn't have any money. Walters was also there and said to Mrs. Revel, "I don't have any money either." He then turned to Sarah and said, "As soon as she is gone I will kill you stone dead if you don't give me the 3s 6d you have stolen from me." Mrs. Revel thought it would be better to leave the money until next week and left.

Shortly afterwards Mrs. Bradshaw a neighbour came round to see Sarah, Walters answered the door and told her that Sarah had gone out and would be back shortly. Then a little girl called Osborne called round and knocked on the door, she got no reply so she looked through the window. She was horrified to see Sarah laid naked on the hearthrug. She was badly beaten and laid in a pool of blood, she also saw what appeared to be Walters knelt down beside Sarah's feet. The little girl ran off to inform her parents what she had seen.

Meanwhile Walters left the house and at 5.45pm, he went round to a neighbours house and said, "Will you come to round to see my missus, I think that she is dead. He approached a police constable walking the street at West Bergreen. He said to the P.C. "I have been out drinking, I got home and found the naked body of my wife, she has no clothes on and is covered in blood. I do not know what happened, I have just got home."

The constable noticed that Walters had blood on his shirt, this seemed feasible he thought as he had just found his wife. They both went round to the house and found Sarah dead.

Walters was arrested and taken in for questioning, the neighbours and Mrs. Revel came forward and were interviewed. The police had enough to charge Walters with the murder.

He was remanded in custody and appeared at the local Magistrates court where he pleaded not guilty, his next appearance was at the NorthEastern Assizes in Leeds in March before Mr. Justice Walton. Mr. Stachan and Mr. C.F. Lowenthal prosecuted the case and Mr. H.T. Waddy and Mr. Courts Trotter defended the prisoner.

The prosecution case was that; Walters and Sarah had both been drunk, she owed him some money but couldn't pay it back so Walters set about her and murdered her in circumstances of peculiar atrocity.

The prosecution called Mrs. Revel and Mrs. Bradshaw to the witness box to give evidence. After hearing their accounts of that afternoon, they called 3 public house licensee's who were from the 3 public houses which Walters had said in his defence that he had visited. Not one of these men could recognise him as being in their pub on the afternoon or early evening of the 23rd December 1905.

The case didn't add up the prosecution said. "He was at home around 5pm seen by the fish hawker, around 5.30pm Mrs Bradshaw spoke to him on his doorstep, and at 5.40pm his wife was dead. How could he have managed to leave the house at 5.30pm visit 3 pubs, drink ale and then get back home for 5.40pm?"

Walters defence was that he had met the woman 3 months previously, they were generally speaking on relatively good terms. During the last two weeks she had taken to drink, he had left the house that afternoon and gone to 3 public houses, when he returned he found the door shut. He went round the back and called out Sarah, there was no answer, and he saw her laid on the floor with a pool of blood gushing from her head. He went closer and lifted her head. That's when he got blood on his shirt. He ran to the neighbours and then found a police constable.

The jury returned the verdict of guilty after only 30 minutes of deliberation, they recommended mercy due to Walters being drunk and incapable condition at the time.

The judge spoke to Walters and said that it was a murder on a frenzy of brutal passion and sentenced then him to death.

He was taken away to Wakefield prison for the first execution to be performed at the prison. The execution chamber had been completed with previous summer; it stood beside C block, but within the prison walls.

Walters had visits from his parents, 3 brothers and his sister along with the Bishop of Wakefield Dr. Eden. W.A. Pierrepoint and his brother arrived at the prison on the 9th April 1906 to prepare for the execution the next day.

Walters was pinioned and walked to the gallows quite composed, he had throughout his confinement been resigned to his fate. He didn't make any statement or remark before the bolt was drawn.

Around 1000 people congregated outside the prison, a majority were woman, all they could see was the top of the execution chamber and hear the ringing of the bells after the execution, perhaps this was enough to satisfy their curiosity.

Chapter 50 - Middlesbrough Strangler

25 year old Thomas Acomb Mouncer lived in lodgings at 35 Olive Street, Middlesbrough, with his on and off girl friend Elizabeth Baldwin. The couple had only lived together for a week this time round, after just recently deciding to get back together. Elizabeth had been living previously with a man called Cram, but this relationship broke up and she moved to a house at belonging to Mr. Gibson.

Mouncer knew about the relationship that Elizabeth had with Cram, and he mentioned to Mr. Gibson before moving Elizabeth, if she ever went with another man, especially Cram he would kill her.

On the night of the 12th May 1906, the couple went drinking to two public houses, while in the course of the evening they happened to come across Elizabeth's old flame Cram. This didn't go down too well with Mouncer, especially when Cram commented to him, that she was the best woman in the world. Mouncer kept quiet, not intending on getting into an argument.

They left the public house and headed back to their lodgings belonging to Mrs. Pattison. They seemed to be on quite good terms when they arrived back at the house and took themselves off to bed without more to do.

At about 12.30am the Mrs. Pattison heard a noise coming from the room that the couple occupied, she quietly went to the door and listened. She heard Elizabeth say, "Oh Tom, don't!" She tapped on the door and asked if everything was ok, there was no reply, so she knocked louder and asked if Elizabeth was ill? Mouncer replied that she was ok. Immediately afterwards Mrs. Pattison heard gargling sounds coming from the room, although she was still suspicious couldn't do anymore and took herself off to bed.

Just after 4am another lodger heard their door open, foot stepson the staircase and then the front door close. Mouncer had left the house and was walking the streets, he came across a police sergeant in Corporation Street at around 6.30 that morning, and he approached him, the Sgt. said, "What's up?"

Mouncer replied. "I have strangled Elizabeth Coleman, (Coleman being the name which Elizabeth was generally known as) we live at 35 Olive Street, we were drunk last night and I strangled her. Here is the key go and look yourself, she is laid on the bed."

Mouncer was arrested and the police went round to the house in Olive Street, Elizabeth was dead, laid on the bed and had been strangled like Mouncer had told them.

He was charged with murder and appeared at the NorthEastern circuit Assizes at York in front of Mr. Justice Grantham. Mr. A. W. Bairstow and Mr. J. Andrews prosecuted the case on behalf of the director of prosecutions and Mr. E. Shortt defended Mouncer.

Medical evidence showed that Elizabeth had been strangled, there were no other marks on the dead body to suggest that there had been a struggle.

Mouncer was put on the stand to give his evidence he said that; He and Elizabeth had been drinking on the Saturday night, in fact they had been drinking all week. When they got home from the pub, they had started arguing, she told him the Cram was a better man and then rushed at him with an open knife. He managed to take the knife from her and threw her upon the bed, putting the knife on the bedside table. He thought she was asleep, but when he woke in the middle of the night she was black in the face. It was then that he realised that he had killed her, so he rushed out and found the police sergeant.

The police sergeant was recalled to the stand and confirmed that there was no sign of a struggle in the bedroom, there were no marks on the deceased to suggest a struggle, nor were there any marks in the prisoner when he was arrested. He also said that there was knife found at all in the room.

Mr. Shortt contended that these facts would warrant a verdict of manslaughter only. The jury retired to consider the verdict, and returned shortly later and found the prisoner guilty of murder and commended him to mercy.

The judge on passing the death sentence said that, "He would not speak of his earlier life, but could not help feeling that was which brought him to his fate. The recommendation of mercy would be passed onto the proper quarter." He then sentenced Mouncer the death.

Mouncer was taken away to Wakefield prison and waited for Henry and Thomas Pierrepoint the appointed executioners to execute him on the 9th August 1906.

Chapter 51 – Last Journey

Hull couple, Thomas aged 29 and Gertrude Siddle aged 22 started of married life around 1904, They seemed happy at first, but things started to take a downward turn. Thomas started drinking far too much which undoubtedly resulted in arguments between the couple.

Thomas was a bricklayer and earned quite a reasonable amount of money, he was able to spend money drinking, pay the household bills and give his wife money.

He soon got into the habit of getting drunk every night, not going to work the next day, so at the end of the week he would be a day short in his pay packet. The spiral effect had started; one day off work soon led to two, then three.

Before long he wasn't working, just drinking. The bills started mounting up, the housekeeping money soon dried up, and the small amount of money that he earned he spent drinking, and only gave Gertrude a small amount for her and his son's needs.

She decided that she had had enough and left him, moving in to a friend's house. On March 3rd 1908 she applied for a separation order, which was granted and Siddle was ordered to pay her 7s 6d for her upkeep and also for their son Harry.

It did not take long for Siddle to get himself into arrears with the maintenance; he was taken back to court for non-payment, the magistrates telling him, if he didn't pay the arrears he would be sent to prison.

On the 9th of June 1908, he made a visit to where Gertrude was staying; she came to the door to see what he wanted. He said, "I am going up the hill for 30 days for not paying what I should pay." While pointing to the Hull prison, up in the distance.

He then noticed that she was wearing a ring on her finger and enquired who had given it to her. She said her friend the landlady had lent her it to wear.

He replied, "Some bloke has given it you, who is it?"

She again told him it was the landlady, but he was not having any of it.

Meanwhile the landlady had heard what was happening and had walked round and stood behind Siddle, keeping her distance but close enough for Siddle to know that she was there.

Siddle said, "Goodbye Gertie, I shall shake hands with you, then I am off." He moved forward towards her.

Immediately Gertrude screamed out, "Oh Mabel!" Then she fell to the floor, into the corner of the hallway.

Her throat had been cut with the razor that Siddle had been carrying in his jacket pocket. Blood was rushing everywhere.

Mrs. Felcay the landlady screamed. Her husband was at work so she ran out into the street screaming, "Murder."

Siddle calmly walked out of the garden and into the street, by now a crowd had gathered to see what was going on. Siddle threw the razor over some railings and strolled down the street.

Police constable Taylor arrested him very shortly afterwards. Siddle said to him, "I am not going to run away. I give myself up for murdering my wife." He was and taken back to the house in Tyne Street, Hull.

As they got to the railings where Siddle had thrown the razor over, a little boy passed it to the constable. Siddle said to P.C. Taylor, "Take care of that, that's what I did it with."

Gertrude Siddle was taken to the Hull Infirmary, where she died 15 minutes after being admitted. The doctors battled to save her life, but the wound was so severe they didn't stand a chance.

Thomas Siddle was charged with murder and after the preliminary proceedings he appeared at the NorthEastern Assizes at

York before Mr. Justice Grantham. Mr. Bruce Williamson and Mr. Horace Marshall prosecuted to case and Mr. Rowan-Hamilton defended Siddle.

The prosecution's case was that, Siddle went to the house, pulled a razor and slit Gertrude Siddle's throat, in front of a witness.

A statement was read out in court, it said, "I saw my wife on that day, I tried to persuade her to come back to me. I produced the razor merely to alarm my wife. I did not remember anything until I saw my wife with her throat slit."

The Director of Public Prosecutions produced a letter from the prison doctor relating to the condition of the prisoner. Mr. Williamson stated that he had no intention of calling Dr. Horton to the stand, so the evidence has no bearing in the trial.

Mr. Rowan-Hamilton said that it would show the state of mind of the prisoner near the time of the murder. The learned judge allowed the letter to be read in court and said. "From whatever cause it was lamentable that in a case of such gravity Dr. Horton should not be present to assist the court."

Mr. Rowan-Hamilton read the letter;

Sir, On reception Thomas Siddle showed evidence of chronic alcoholism. Since his reception his condition has improved, and he is now well and of sound mind.
Yours obediently.
E.H. Horton.

The defence was that Siddle had been drinking heavily throughout the previous weeks and months. He was drunk at the time of the murder, but he didn't intend on murdering his wife.

The jury retired to consider their verdict, and returned a short while later and found the prisoner guilty of murder. Mr. Justice Grantham sentenced Siddle to the death penalty in the usual way and ordered him to be taken away.

The crimes behind the hangings

Siddle was taken to the cells and then later escorted to the train station to board the train to Hull. When they arrived in Hull a cab was waiting to transport him the final few miles to the Hull prison.

A huge crowd had gathered at the train station, Siddle was jeered, booed and many rocks were thrown at his direction. Comments were heard that this was going to be his final journey.

He arrived safely at Hull and was put in the condemned cell to wait for Albert Pierrepoint to execute him.

4TH August 1908, Thomas Siddle ate a hearty breakfast; he was then pinioned and led to the gallows, smiling. Death was recorded as instantaneous.

Chapter 52 – The Reference

The firm of Fieldhouse and Jowett, Listerhills, Bradford, was a large employer in 1908, their mill, dyed cloth for the cotton trade, Thomas Wilkinson was a 56 year old cashier for the firm. He usually worked out of the office at Listerhills, apart from on a Friday morning when, he worked out of a small office in Swaine Street, Bradford.

This made it easier for him to leave home on a Friday, go directly to the bank, pay the week's cheques in, and draw money out for the staff wages. He would then go to Swaine Street, put the money in pay packets for each employee, which they would collect later that day.

Around dinner time on the 31st July 1908 a member of staff from the mill came down to the office, They gave Thomas some cheques, one for the wages and the other to pay in. Thomas put the cheques in his pocket, and then home went for dinner. He left shortly after 2pm and headed back to the office, before intending on going to the bank.

Shortly after 2.30pm Thomas was found battered and unconscious with a poker in the office. The poker, blood stained was laid next to him. The police were informed and Thomas was rushed to the Bradford Infirmary, where he later died, without regaining consciousness.

The cheques that he had been given were still in his pocket, his gold watch and chain was still there, along with a small amount of loose change in silver and coppers.

The police interviewed other people in the office and it was established that in the morning he had received a telephone call from someone and had arranged a meeting with them around 2.15pm.

A witness who worked near the office came forward and said that they had seen Mr. Wilkinson talking to a man on the steps of the office around 2.30, then he went back in closely followed by the second man who was carrying a long thin parcel. The man was wearing a brown suit.

A girl Miss Craven was passing the office shortly after 2.30pm; she had a groan, and saw a man wearing a brown suit, standing near the door, his hands was covered in blood.

Isaac Pollard told the police that he was outside the office, and saw two men talking, one of them went inside while the other stood on the steps. He said he was having a bit of bother, he went into the building and came out a couple of minutes later, rubbing his hands, I couldn't see anything on his hands.

The man again went into the office. When he came out he was breathless and said the bother is sorted. He left and walked down the street. He wasn't carrying the long parcel that he had before going in the office.

The whole police force in Bradford was put on alert to catch the murderer and a description of a man was circulated:

About 40 years old, 5ft 10in tall; stoutly built; dressed well in brown mixture suit, and wearing a double gold chain.

Detective sergeant Knowles received information regarding the identity and address of the man they wanted to question. At 5am on the Saturday 1st August he went to a house in Bradford, knocked on the door, a man answering the description answered the door.

Sgt. Knowles cautioned the man and asked him to accompany him to the police station.

The man answered, "I know nothing about it, but I will come with you."

This man John William Ellwood had worked for the same firm for 14 years, but he had left 8 months previous and was now working as an agent for the British Homes Insurance Society.

The police searched his house and found a brown suit with a green stripe in it. The elbow on the right coat sleeve had traces of blood, and also the trousers contained marks of blood.

Isaac Pollard, and the girl that saw the man outside the office, were taken to the police station and identified Ellwood as the man who they had seen the previous afternoon.

Ellwood was charged with the murder, he was asked if he had anything to say in reply to the charge, he remained silent.

The Leeds Assizes was the venue for the trial, Mr. Justice Pickford presided over the case, Mr. C .F. Lowenthal and Mr. Frank Newbolt prosecuted and Mr. Charles Mellor, Mr. J. J. Wright and Mr. Geoffrey Ellis defended Ellwood.

The prosecution case was that: Ellwood had worked for the firm for 14 years, he had been dismissed due to an argument with one of the Jowett's, his sister was married to the manager a Mr. Jowett. Since his dismissal he was struggling to make a decent living, so he decided to take revenge.

Ellwood knew the routine of Thomas Wilkinson on wage days, he bought a poker from second hand shop, went to Swaine Street to rob Mr. Wilkinson.

Unfortunately Thomas Wilkinson had not been to the bank, so Ellwood beat him with the poker and stole his personal money. He then went outside for a moment before returning into the office and continued the beating. He was seen leaving the building by witnesses, with blood on his hands, and on his clothes.

Evidence was called from witnesses who saw Ellwood outside the office, and then a man called Mason was called to the stand.

Mr. Mason's evidence was such; He had been in the company of Ellwood on that afternoon, Ellwood was wearing a brown suit and a double watch chain. They had a drink together at a public house on Manchester Road at around 1.30 – 2pm. They parted company, Ellwood going in the direction of Swaine Street.

Mr. Ellis gave evidence. "I own a second hand shop about 300 yards away from Swaine Street, on the afternoon of 31st July a man came into the shop wearing a brown suit, this man bought a second hand poker for 3d. The man who bought the poker is in the prisoner, whom I have known for a while."

The defence cross-examined Ellis. "At the police station you could not identify the purchaser of the poker. At the inquest you were still unable to identify the purchaser of the poker, now you tell this court, that the man was Mr. Ellwood, whom you have known for a considerable time. Who was it?"

"I have no doubt about it, it was the prisoner. I wanted to be absolutely certain, that's why I did not identify him at the police station or the inquest." Replied Ellis.

"When did you come to the conclusion that this was the man? You know this man's neck is in jeopardy and I want you to be careful, and it greatly depends on your evidence too."

"It was about Saturday!" Answered Ellis. "I wanted to recall everything fact in my mind before he felt certain in a such a serious matter, and before he swore to it."

"Since the inquest has anyone on the part of the police spoken to you about this matter?"

"No, sir not on either side."

Dr. Enrich who conducted the post mortem described Thomas's injuries. "In my opinion death was due to a compound fracture of the skull and laceration if the brain. The injuries must have been caused by frequent applications of direct violence. At least ten heavy blows must have been struck, and at least two of these were sufficient to cause death. A poker was a likely instrument to have caused the injuries, if used with considerable strength. The injuries could not have been self-inflicted or accidental. The fatal injuries were in all probability inflicted while Wilkinson was on the ground. The wounds substantiated the allegation of two attacks."

Dr. Wrangham the police surgeon said. "I found 12 stains on the front of the brown suit worn by Ellwood. 10 stains were on the right sleeve and 2 stains on the trousers. On microscopic examination, they were found to be animal blood, they were fresh and corresponded with the stains on the office wall and the poker."

Mrs. Wilkinson gave evidence that Thomas had sent a letter to Ellwood that was delivered on the Saturday, asking that Ellwood phone him when he was in the office on Friday, to arrange an appointment to discuss the reference that Ellwood had asked him to submit on his behalf.

Thomas's secretary gave evidence that a telephone called was made to Thomas on the Friday morning and she heard an appointment for someone to visit the office in the afternoon. She didn't know who had made the call, or who had arranged to visit.

The prosecution summed up the case to the jury, the evidence they said. "Pointed to only one conclusion. That conclusion was that Thomas William Ellwood had murdered Thomas Wilkinson in one of the most brutal murders possible.

The defence after outlining the case to the jury called on Ellwood to give evidence.

Ellwood said, "On the Friday I was wearing a brown suit, the same suit which I have on now. I met Mason for a drink in Manchester Road; I left him and got home about 2pm. I left again around 2.20pm, with some money that I collected from home. I went to the public house where I paid the landlady some money for the never never club that she runs. The public house is about a mile in the opposite direction to Swaine Street and I was there at 2.45pm. I did not go to Swaine Street, I did not buy a poker on Manchester Road and I did not see Thomas that day. The last time I saw Thomas was the 27th July."

"What about receiving a letter from Mr. Wilkinson?" Asked Mr. Mellor.

"Yes I got a letter from him on the Saturday, I destroyed it, but it referred to an appointment which I had applied for, it did not mention going to see him, or him wanting me to make a telephone call to him."

"Can you explain how you managed to have traces of blood on you suit?"

"On Tuesday before the murder, my little boy who is just 4 year old fell down in the yard and cut himself. I picked the child up, his nose was bleeding and I got some drops of blood on my clothes."

Mrs. Ellwood and also her brother Gregory, who lived at the same address, corroborated the account of the little boy falling.

The defence then summed up the evidence to the jury, "We have proved that Mr. Ellwood was nowhere near the murder scene that day, he had no motive, in fact the death of Mr. Wilkinson meant that he wouldn't get the reference which he required. The verdict of not guilty is the only possible verdict."

It was then the turn of the judge to sum up the evidence to the jury.

He said. "The kernel of the case for the prosecution was the identification of the prisoner by Mason, Pollard and the girl Mary Craven. This was not the only question in the case, but it was the most important. If the man whom those witnesses saw was the prisoner and their identification was right, the story of the prisoner and his wife must be rejected, and they could hardly escape the conclusion that the prisoner was the man who committed the murder. But if they thought there was any reasonable doubt as to the correctness of the identification of the man who was seen standing in Swaine Street, and spoke to Pollard, they would probably feel it their duty to acquit him."

The jury after an hour of deliberating the case returned back to the court and found the prisoner guilty of murder. The judge passed the death sentence, and then the prisoner was taken down.

The court of criminal appeal was asked by Mr. Ellis for leave to appeal the sentence issued by Justice Pickford, on the grounds that facts were disclosed in court that entitled the prisoner to have an appeal. The judge's carefully reviewed the case, and on the 20th November they refused leave to appeal.

Henry Pierrepoint executed 44 year old John William Ellwood on the 3rd December 1908 at Armley jail.

Chapter 53 – A Christmas Murder

Ernest Hutchinson aged 24 was a butcher for a while, he got injured at work and received a pension from this former employers in the amount of 10 shillings every week. He didn't have to work so he just spent his time going out drinking.

He met Hannah, a working girl in 1907; she was married but had been separated from her husband for a few years. Hutchinson started a relationship with Hannah, and they both decided to live together in April 1908, provided that she changed her ways. They moved into the house of Hutchinson at Great Albion Street, Halifax, and almost immediately the arguments started.

Christmas Eve 1908, Hutchinson went out to celebrate with some friends, they went to a couple of pubs, and he went home around 11pm. Not long after he returned home the neighbours heard the sound of breaking glass.

Mrs. Catherine Kershaw one of the neighbours heard the glass break; she went to the front door of Hutchinson's and heard an argument. She saw a hand come through the paper blinds and smash another window, then a figure fall to the floor. She rushed home to tell her husband, and then they both went back to the house.

When they got there, all was quiet at the Hutchinson's home, the door was locked, and what looked like blood was running from underneath the door. Mrs. Kershaw decided to leave things until the morning and then go back round.

Christmas morning and all was quiet, no movement at all in the house. Fifteen year old Thomas McCrevy who lived with his father round the corner at New Bank, was out having a walk. He walked down the street and saw the daughter of Hannah stood in her bedroom window, she knocked and summoned him over. She was crying and looked distraught. Thomas put his hand through the broken window of the door and opened it. He immediately saw Hannah, sat upright in the hallway, blood was everywhere, but she was not moving. She was cold, white and obviously dead.

Hutchinson was sat on the stairs; he had a gaping wound to his neck.

Thomas ran out of the house and summoned a man who was passing by. Arthur Kershaw, put Hutchinson in a chair and covered him up, he had lost a lot of blood. He told Thomas to run and fetch a policeman and a doctor. Then he went upstairs, on going into the bedroom; there was a very strong smell of gas.

The gas tap had been turned on full and the pipe that should have been connected to the fire was missing. In its place was a small rubber pipe that was not connected to anything, allowing the gas to escape into the bedroom. He turned off the gas tap and opened the windows to allow the gas to escape. He then carried Hannah's daughter down and out of the house, taking her to a neighbour's so she would be looked after.

The police came along with a doctor, Hutchinson was taken to the local hospital for surgery to his neck and Hannah was taken to the mortuary. Hutchinson made a full recovery and then was charged with the murder. He appeared at the Leeds Assizes in front of Mr. Justice Coleridge. Mr. Bruce Williamson and Mr. O. J. Robinson prosecuted him, and Mr. S. Flemming defended him.

The prosecution called numerous witnesses to show that Hutchinson regularly assaulted Hannah. Hannah was not the perfect woman and they agreed she had a temper, she enjoyed drinking and was often quarrelsome afterwards. She also enjoyed the attention of different men.

They also showed evidence that Hutchinson had beaten Hannah on the 17th November last year, he had been arrested but was only charged with using obscene language.

They summed their evidence up to the jury;

"The case is and open and shut case." They said. "Hutchinson went out on Christmas Eve, he came home a little after 11pm in a drunken state. A fight started between the couple, a window got smashed, and in a rage he picked up a knife and slit Hannah's throat. He then turned the knife on himself; the wound to his throat was not fatal, so he turned the gas tap on in the bedroom, either to gas himself or to cause an explosion. The verdict of guilty of murder was the only verdict that could be reached."

Mr. Flemming for the defence called Hutchinson to the stand. "Did you hit Hannah on the 17th November last year?" he asked

"Yes, I came home and caught her letting a man out of the back door, I saw red and slapped her, that was all. We argued about the man and I was arrested for using obscene language," He replied.

He was then asked to account in his own words what had happened on Christmas Eve.

"I went down to the public house, like I have done every Christmas Eve. When I left the pub I joined in with some carol singers outside in the street. Then I went home. I saw Hannah letting someone out of the house again, so I asked her what she was doing with that fellow that has just left. She shouted at me, what has it got to do with you. We sat down and had a glass of beer, I asked her again about the bloke that had just left. She said she would make the kid pay for telling on her. She grabbed the razor from the drawer and set of upstairs to get the kid."

"I grabbed her and pulled her back. That's when she cut my throat, I lost my temper and we started fighting for 2 or 3 minutes. I don't know how I managed to get a knife in my hand, but I hit her with the knife. I don't know where I hit her, but I did. She then ran over towards the door and grabbed some money out of the flowerpot. She smashed the window in the door and then fell to the ground. I felt faint from the cut to my throat so I went upstairs to the kid and laid down. I don't remember anymore, until the next morning when I saw the lad open the door and walk in."

Mr. Flemming made a strong appeal to the jury to find the prisoner not guilty. He said. "He had brought her out of a loose life, she was unfaithful to him and was deceiving him. A quarrel started and in the heat of the moment she hit him with a razor. He retaliated but unfortunately her wounds were fatal. This is a case of manslaughter and not murder, it was not premeditated, but was the result of events that had gone badly wrong."

The jury found the prisoner guilty of murder. The judge asked Hutchinson if he had anything to say. He replied, "I did not mean to kill her, I shall appeal the verdict."

The judge passed the sentence of death. Hutchinson was hoping and waiting for a reprieve while he was in Wakefield prison.

On the 1st March 1909, he received a visit from the prisoner governor telling him that a reprieve had not been granted and he would be going to meet Henry Pierrepoint at the gallows the next day. On hearing the news he said, "Well I can only die once."

Hutchinson appeared to have gained 17lbs in weight since his confinement. He had been to the chapel on the Sunday before the execution and participated in the singing out loud of Onward Christian Soldiers.

On the morning of his execution, he had slept well and he ate a hearty breakfast before enjoying smoking his pipe. He shook hands with the governor and wardens as he was led to the gallows.

A crow flew onto the roof of the scaffold, as Hutchinson was being led up the stairs, it seemed to be watching the proceedings, flying away only as the bell stuck 9am, and the bolt being drawn.

Chapter 53 – Crock's Yard

Thomas Mead aged 34 and 38 year old Clara Howell lived together at Crooks Yard off West Street, Leeds. They had been together for seven years and the local neighbourhood was well aware of the volatile relationship, which the couple led. Clara was often to be seen bruised and battered. Black eyes and bruised ribs were a regular sight on this poor woman.

The house, in which they lived, was sparsely furnished; most of the meagre earnings that Mead made as a labourer at the local gas-work's, were spent on nights out at the local pub.

The shouting and arguing of the couple once again disturbed the residents of crooks yard on the 27th November 1908, things seemed to be getting out of hand and the police were called to the house.

They arrived and calmed the situation down leaving in the early hours of the morning. Things again flared up when the police had left. More shouting and sounds of breaking furniture was to be heard for a while then a deadly silence.

Nine o'clock the next morning Mead left the house and spoke to a neighbour who was washing her front step. She asked where Clara was and Mead replied that she had gone to visit her mother for a couple of days.

Mrs. Whittaker, the neighbour thought that this was strange, as she knew Clara well, staying away from home for any length of time was something that Clara never did. However nothing else was said and Mead carried on walking down the street

Mead then arrived at the local pub for a drink where he had arranged to meet a friend called John Prenderville; the drinks started to flow and later that day a fight broke out and the landlord ejected Mead.

He then turned up at another friend's house, his friend's daughter Margaret Shuttleworth answered the door, Mead asked if he could sleep on the sofa for the night. Margaret knew that Mead was a close friend of her father Mick Robinson so she allowed Mead to sleep there.

In the morning when Margaret asked Mead why he had slept on the sofa the previous night and not gone home, Mead said that, "He and Clara had an argument, which had got out of hand, he had blackened her eyes and then killed her."

Meanwhile at Crook's Yard Sarah Whittaker was concerned that Clara had not returned home from her mothers so she summoned the police.

A police constable called Garbutt arrived and accompanied Sarah across the street to Clara's home. They knocked on the door and got no reply so P.C. Garbutt borrowed a ladder and climbed up to the bedroom window.

He could see a pile of rags in the corner of the room, using his baton he smashed the window and climbed through to the bedroom. Under the pile of rags, he found the dead body of Clara Howell, naked and badly beaten.

The conversation between Margaret Shuttleworth and Mead was interrupted when a neighbour rushed round to the house saying,

"The police had found Clara and she had been murdered." Mead panicked, grabbed his coat and hat then bolted out of the door, running to another friend's house, this time in Chadwick Place. It was at this house that he was arrested on the Monday night, transported to the police station at Wortley, Leeds, where he was charged with murder.

Mead was to stand trial for the murder of Clara Howell on 10th February 1909 before Mr. Justice Coleridge. Mr. J.W. Jardine represented the accused and Mr. Bruce Williamson appeared for the crown.

Mr. Williamson stated that Mead and Clara Howell lived together in what could only be described was squalor, the only furniture in the living room being a wooden chair and this had been smashed on the night of the murder.

He went on to say that Clara had been found naked and badly beaten, she had numerous cuts to her face, head and body. Her nose had been broken; a hard blow to the lower part of her stomach had ruptured her intestine and killed her.

A broken blood stained broom handle had been found downstairs along with blood splattered on the walls and floor, this suggesting that the murder had been carried out downstairs, then the body stripped and carried upstairs to the bedroom.

John Prenderville, Mead's friend said, "He had met Mead in the pub the day after the murder and Mead had told him that Clara had taken some money out of his pocket, he had hit her, causing her to fall over. He carried her to bed where she had died a few minutes later."

The landlord of the public house in evidence said that Mead had been in his public house, the night after the murder. He had been involved in a fight, so he ejected him, Mead had shouted to him, let me back in so I can do him, I have done one already, take the key and go and look.

The defence's case was that Mead had been drunk and therefore not responsible for his actions. He was not capable of understanding the results of his actions and consequently he was guilty of manslaughter and not murder.

The judge in summing up told the jury that, "Although an insane person was not liable to the same consequences, and was not judged by the same standard as a sane one. Yet if he was suffering from a temporary insanity caused by the accused own voluntary act in getting drunk, the legal doctrine stated that drunkenness was no excuse for a crime. He who is guilty of any crime whatever through voluntary drunkenness shall be punished for it equally as much as if he had been sober. The defence was not a defence of insanity therefore if the jury found that Mead had killed Clara Howell then they had to return a verdict of murder."

The jury retired to consider their verdict and returned shortly afterwards and found the accused guilty of murder.

The judge sentenced Mead to death by hanging and he was taken to the condemned cell to await the arrival of Messrs Pierrepoint and Ellis.

The defence lodged an appeal with the court of appeal, on Feb 23rd 1909, after considering the facts of the case, three Lord Justices dismissed the appeal and Mead was to hang.

On the morning of 12th March 1909 at Armley jail, Mead ate a hearty breakfast then prepared himself with dignity to be pinioned by the executioners. He did not speak as he was led to the gallows. His death was instantaneous.

Chapter 55 – The Painter.

Walter Davis aged 37 was born in Worcester in the Midlands; he was a painter by trade and worked around the North of England. He met Hester Richards while he was working in Northallerton, in North Yorkshire and the couple started a relationship. He then found work in Leeds and then Ilkley and moved, taking Hester with him.

Things seemed to be good between the couple; he worked hard and looked after Hester rather well at this time. Unfortunately the job he was doing in Ilkley finished, there wasn't much work around at the time.

He was at a loss of where to try next to find work. That's when Hester decided that she was going to go back to Middlesbrough.

What Davis didn't know at that time, was that she was going back to live with her estranged husband.

Matters were discussed and a plan was made, Hester would go back home, and a couple of weeks later Davis would follow.

She would introduce him to her husband as her cousin, everything would be fine, they could live in the same house and continue the affair when James Richards her husband was at work.

Off she went; Davis followed a short time afterwards. Things worked out for a while, but Davis was jealous about the time that Hester spent with Richards so he announced on the 29th March, that he had found work and was going to Birmingham the following day.

Money was a little tight, because Davis was Hester's cousin, James reluctantly agreed to pawn his best suit to pay the train fare. He was assured that Davis would send the money back out of his first pay packet.

The following morning James and another lodger left the house to go to work, Davis and Hester were alone in the house, Davis was seen to leave around 9am carrying his bags and heading towards the train station.

A lodger came home around 11am that morning, Hester was nowhere to be seen, so she entered her bedroom, Hester was laid on the bed, dead, her head had been battered in and there was blood splattered everywhere.

The police were called and a search of the house conducted. A bloodstained hammer was found in the kitchen cupboard, the police doctor was quite sure that this was the weapon used to murder Hester Richards.

Walter Davis was the last person to see Hester alive, the police were anxious to question him.

Davis hadn't gone to Birmingham, nor had he gone to any friends or family that the police knew about, they interviewed all Hester's relatives, it became quite clear that Davis was not a cousin at all.

A nation-wide manhunt started to find him. Handbills were printed, his description was given to all the police forces in England, and even a small reward was offered for his apprehension.

Davis was eventually caught on the outskirts of Blyth on the 17th April. He was taken to Middlesbrough for questioning and eventually charged with wilful murder and remanded in custody until the court hearing in York.

Mr. C. F. Lawrence and Mr. Hedley prosecuted the case and Mr. G. F. Mortimer defended the prisoner in front of Mr. Justice Bucknill.

Mr. Lawrence outlined the prosecution case to the jury, then called the police constable who arrested Davis to give evidence.

The police constable said, "When I arrested Davis for the murder he said to me, I know the job you mean, but you will have to prove it. Later on he said that he has been fed up since the job happened and has not slept since."

Mr. Richards gave evidence, "I did not know about the affair, if I did I would have gone at him like a mad dog. When I first met Davis I thought him a wrong one."

Davis shouted from the dock, "It's the other way around!"

The judge interrupted, "No! No! You must not do this. If I were you Davis I would let him give evidence."

"But its hard for me!" replied Davis.

The questing of Mr. Richards continued, Davis interrupting whenever he felt the need to. The judge finally had enough he said, "If you do not shut up, I will send you down to the cells for contempt of court, you will have to wait there until the verdict is reached."

Mr. Mortimer put Davis on the stand; he remained composed and seemed aware of the seriousness of the crime which he was charged with.

"Quite straightly, Mr. Davis did you have anything to do with Hester Richards death?" he asked.

Davis in reply, "No sir I did not!"

"What did happen that morning Mr. Davis?"

"After Richards and the lodger went to work, I left and went to the post office and then to the shop to get a steak for Richards' tea. Hester also asked me to bring back 6d of whiskey, which I did. I got back to the house and found Hester battered to death in the bedroom. I did not know what to do so I just left. I did not make any statement to the police like they have said in evidence that is all lies. I am innocent, I have not killed anyone."

The judge summed up the evidence to the jury; they left the court to deliberate, then returned the verdict of guilty.

The judge passed the death sentence in the usual way. Davis as he was led away shouted that he was innocent of the charges and he would appeal the verdict.

On the 25th June 1909, the court of criminal appeal dismissed the prisoner's application of leave to appeal. Davis was executed on the 9th July, Henry and Thomas Pierrepoint were the executioners.

Chapter 56 – The Sister In Law

John Freeman aged 46 lived at Hull, he lodged with his brother Robert and Roberts wife Florence Lily Freeman aged 30. All 3 were drinking together on the 28th August 1909, was started off as a few drinks turned in a major argument and then murder.

Lilly was talking to her Robert in the kitchen, he was heard by a neighbour Mrs. Mary Clark say, "You have been with him again." Lilly called him a liar. A quarrel started between the three of them, which then resulted in a fight between the two brothers.

Mary Clark heard the sound of breaking furniture, a table being overturned and the smashing of crockery. This was a usual Saturday night at the Freeman's home so she didn't do anything to help. The next sound that Mary heard was Lilly screaming "Murder." in the back garden shortly followed by, "Look blood."

Marine engineer Patrick Geraghty heard the commotion going on from the street behind the house, he ran to the back gate and saw John Freeman go up to Lilly, who was by the back door step, lift her head up and made a slashing movement at her throat. Lilly then fell into his arms. Freeman laid her on the floor and went back inside and carried on the fighting with his brother.

Mary after hearing the scream coming from No4 went round into the garden. She saw Lilly laid face down, and the sounds of a violent fight continuing from inside.

The police were soon alerted and Sgt. Boyes along with two police constables came to the house, they heard the sound of a fight going on inside the house, the front door was locked so they went round the back. Lilly was laid by the back door, her lips were quivering, and blood was coming from a wound in her throat and in her chest, she was unable to speak to say what had happened. Sgt. Boyes left the 2 constables outside to attend to Lilly then he went inside.

As he entered the room that looked like a bombsite, with over turned furniture and broken pots and ornaments strewed everywhere. Robert had just managed to get a grip on his brother and was attempting to hold him down. John however was struggling violently, as well as shouting and swearing. Sgt. Boyes managed to separate the pair, and get John Freeman onto the sofa. Both the men were cut and covered in blood, and both seemed to be intoxicated. Sgt. Bowes asked what had gone on.

John Freeman replied by swearing at him and then said, "I hope that she is dead." Which he repeated several times.

Sgt. Bowes sent for transport to take Lilly and Robert to the Hull Royal Infirmary and John Freeman was taken to the police station. Dr. Roberts the casualty house surgeon at the hospital, pronounced Lilly dead, and Robert was detained suffering from a severe cut to the right eye. The next morning Robert could not remember anything that had happened the previous night, he remembered finishing work at the Queen Elizabeth dock in Hull and then going home.

John Freeman was charged with the murder of Florence Lilly Freeman. He pleaded not guilty at the preliminary hearings. His only defence was that he was so drunk that he did not know what he was doing.

He appeared at the Assizes at York on the 19th November 1909 in front of Mr. Justice Bucknill. The jury found him guilty of murder, he was sent to Hull prison to the condemned cell. Henry Pierrepoint assisted by John Ellis executed him on the morning of the 7th December 1909.

Chapter 57 – The Summons

The Coulson's lived at Springfield Place, Dudley Hill, Bradford. John Coulson aged 32was and engineer's labourer and Jane aged 29 was a weaver at a local mill. Thomas, five, was at school. The marriage was not a happy one, with arguments often being heard coming from the house by the neighbours.

Around the 23rd May 1910, the couple had a major argument resulting in Coulson hitting his wife, causing swelling and bruising to her face.

He went to work the next morning, but his wife went to the police station and made a complaint about the assault that happened the previous evening.

The police issued a summons for him to appear in court. This was served to Coulson at the foundry where he worked.

Coulson was not happy, the summons was going to get withdrawn he told his colleges, he would sort it out when he got home.

He finished his shift, told his mates that he would be speaking to his wife that evening, and he would see them at the usual time tomorrow. He went home, ready to face what he knew would be another blazing argument.

Quarrels were heard again that night, but then the house went silent until the morning. At 6am Jane's friend knocked on the door, as she always did, so they could walk to work together.

There was no answer, the house in complete darkness, the blinds and curtains were drawn. Coulson left the house around 8.30am; he walked the short distance to a pawnbroker and pawned Jane's wedding ring.

Then at 9am a neighbour, Mrs. Fieldhouse went to the house, there was no answer, she tried the door and it was locked.

Coulson turned up for work two hours later; he had with him the summons. When a work mate asked him how he got on getting Jane to withdraw it. Coulson showed him the back of the summons, written on the back was a statement basically saying that he had killed his wife and child, and his dead body would be found in the local dam.

He had also wrote a letter to his sister, telling her that he had cut his wife's throat with a carving knife, and he was going to drowned himself.

His work mates thought that he was kidding and nothing else was said throughout the working day. After work, Couslon went to the public house, he again told everybody about the summons and showed them the statement, which he had written, on the back. He left the pub and went home.

Shortly afterwards there was a knock on the door, Coulson opened it and stood there were police constable Gill and police constable Walker. They went in the house, which was clean and quite orderly. They had heard rumours and were concerned about the whereabouts of his wife and child.

Coulson told them that she had taken the kid to visit family and was due back at the weekend. The police were satisfied that he was telling the truth and they left.

Police constable Walker returned at 11pm that evening. He wanted to speak to Coulson on a matter that was unconnected to his wife and child.

He knocked on the door and got no reply. Because of his previous visit Walker was concerned and broke into the property.

He was totally unprepared to discover the bodies of Jane Coulson and Thomas Coulson. Their throats had been slit; blood was everywhere in the bedroom where they laid. He made a search and found a carving knife that was covered in blood. He walked down the stairs and heard a sound in the kitchen, waiting silently in the hallway he listened.

The outside door had been opened and he could hear the door being locked from the inside, then movement. He rushed through the door with his baton raised.

Coulson was stood there, his clothes dripping wet; he was shocked to see the constable coming at him. He just stood where he was as P.C. Walker, grabbed him and placed him in handcuffs.

"I am arresting you for the murder of your wife Jane Coulson and also the murder of your son Thomas Coulson." Said Walker.

"Its alright, I have just been down to the dam to drowned myself." Replied Coulson.

He was taken to Bradford police station where he was formally charged and remanded in custody.

Mr. Justice Coleridge was the presiding judge at the Leeds Assizes on the 21st July 1910. Mr. Waddy prosecuted the case and Mr. Mockett defended Coulson.

None of the evidence was disputed, it was clear that Couslon was the murderer.

The defence had only one option and that was to try to prove that the prisoner was insane.

They called on Dr. Exley a medical expert who consulted at Armley jail as their witness. Dr. Exley confirmed that at this moment in time, Coulson was perfectly sane. But he could not swear that at the time of the murders, he was either sane or insane.

That was the case of the defence.

The jury had the easy task of finding Coulson guilty of the murders.

The judge said before passing sentence. "You have been convicted of a cruel act involving the murder of your wife and son. I can not see any extenuating circumstances. It was not the first time that you have raised you hand to your wife." He then passed the sentence of death.

Coulson said. "Thank you, that is what I expected."

Then he was led away to the cells below. Henry Pierrepoint arrived at Armley and executed Coulson on the 9th August 1910.

The crimes behind the hangings

Chapter 58 – Was It A Fall?

Boyston Street, Quarry Hill, Hunslet, Leeds was the home of 45 year old Henry Ison and his Girlfriend Mary Jenkin aged 43. On Saturday 23rd July 1910, the couple had been drinking at home.

At around 8pm Mary made a dash out of the house, closely followed by Ison. She managed to run 8 to 10 yards before he caught up with her. He grabbed her and dragged her back to the house.

Mary was struggling to be free from his grip, but as Ison was a short heavily set strong man; Mary didn't have a chance to break free. Annie Northorp was watching from across the street. She didn't do anything to help, as this was a normal occurrence for the couple.

When Ison managed to get Mary to the doorstep, he hit her and kicked her, Mary shouted, "Don't Harry, haven't you done enough?" He pushed her into the house; this was the last time that Mary would be seen alive again.

The next morning Ison went to a Mrs. Bradshaw's house. She was the sister of Mary. He said to her, "Can I have a word? You better get round to Mary now, she is unconscious in front of the fireplace.

Mrs. Bradshaw ran to the house, it was obvious that a struggle had taken place at sometime, and Mary was where Ison said she was.

The police were already at the house, and Ison was arrested, taken into custody and they started gathering evidence from the house, and interviewing neighbours. A poker was recovered and taken away, under suspicion of being the weapon that was used in the assault.

The unconscious Mary was taken to the Leeds Infirmary hospital, Dr. Richardson examined and treated her, but Mary did not recover from her injuries, she died early the next morning without regaining consciousness. Ison was then charged with the murder of Mary Jenkin.

Ison pleaded not guilty at the committal hearings at the Magistrates court. He also pleaded not guilty at the Assizes on the 24th November 1910.

Mr. Shortt K.C. M.P. and Mr. Jardine prosecuted the case and Mr. Charles Mellor defended Ison. The judge was Mr. Justice Hamilton.

Dr. Richardson took the stand to give medical evidence he said. "Mary was admitted to hospital in a deeply unconscious state. She had bruises to her body and 2 or 3 injuries to her head including 1 cut 3 inches long, going from the forehead over the skull. She also died from concussion of the brain. The injuries could have been caused by a poker."

Mr. Mellor in cross-examination asked,

"Could the injuries have been caused by a fall down the steps?"

"Yes, it was possible, but unlikely." Replied Dr. Richardson.

Superintendent from the West Riding police force gave evidence.

"When Ison was charged with the murder, he said, no use talking now, its down to the booze I suppose."

Annie Northorp gave evidence to what see saw taking place in the street that night, she added, "It was a regular occurrence between the couple, they always made up again the next day."

Mr. Mellor called the prisoner to the stand to give evidence in his defence.

"What happened on that Saturday night Henry? Tell us in your own words."

"Well, we had been drinking all day, I gave her a sovereign to fetch some more ale, she came back, and said that someone had taken the sovereign from her. We had a big argument and she ran out of the house. I followed her and dragged her back; I was struggling to get her through the door, as she was very drunk so I give her a kick. She was banging into things, knocking stuff all over. I managed to calm her down and told her it was best to go to bed. She couldn't make the stairs so I carried her up and laid her on the bed. I woke up the next morning and found her laid in front of the fireplace, unconscious. It seemed that she had fallen down the steps and crawled to the hearthrug, where she laid. I ran to get her sister, came back to the house and was arrested. I did not kill her or push her down the stairs."

Mr. Mellor turned to the jury,

"The only witness to what happened, has just given a true and plausible explanation to the events that night. The prosecution case is that Ison hit Mary with the poker they recovered from the house, the poker was in its place at the side of the fire grate. Even more alarmingly the poker did not have traces of blood on it. Dr. Richardson has stated that the injuries could have been caused by a fall down the stairs. Mrs. Northorp said that arguments were a regular event in the household, if Ison was a murderer why had he not done it sooner? We submit, that the death of Mary Jenkin was the result of a tragic accident and not at the hands of the prisoner."

The jury retired to consider their verdict. They came back into court and found the prisoner guilty of murder but recommended mercy.

The judge said to Ison. "Do not count on the recommendation being acted on. Make the most of the time that you have left and prepare for you punishment!"

Ison stood and said. "I have an application to make your lordship. As I have stated before I am innocent of this crime and the sentence is unjust and unfair. The trial was unfair and witnesses on my behalf should have been called."

"What is your request Ison!" interrupted the judge.

"I want to appeal the sentence. I also had 17 shillings and 7d (pence) in my property. I want this money sending to the Leeds Infirmary. I do not want that bad lot drinking my health with my money. They are a bad lot, they will be drinking in 5 minutes anyway."

"Who has the money?" enquired his lordship.

"That lot!" Pointing to the police. "I want the money to go to the hospital that tired to save Mary's life."

"If the police have property belonging to you in their custody, they will dispose of it in the proper way." He then ordered Ison to be taken down.

On 28th December 1910 the Home Secretary refused to intervene with the punishment and Thomas Pierrepoint, conducting his first execution at Armley prison, hanged Ison on the 29th December 1910.

The crimes behind the hangings

Information sources.

The following have been an invaluable source of information.

The times online

Yorkshire Evening Post

Yorkshire Post

Leeds Mercury

Leeds Central Library

Capitalpunishmentuk.org

And many thanks to all the other sources of snippets of information need to compile this book.

Book 2 coming soon 1910 – 1961

Further true accounts of the crimes behind the hangings in Yorkshire.
Including the man hanged in 1954, then someone walked in to Hull police station in 1972 and admitted the crime.

The execution of another man called William Smedley. A man called George Michael and a man called Louis Hamilton.

Also Ethel Lille Major who fed her cheating husband a poisoned corned beef sandwich.

62 remarkable and true crimes that led to the executions.

www.yorkshire-executions.co.uk